A Prayer Book Companion

A Guide to Christian Worship

---✠---

CARL SCOVEL

A Prayer Book Companion:
A Guide to Christian Worship

A layperson's guide to the history and theology of Christian worship.

Published by The Society of King's Chapel
64 Beacon Street
Boston, MA 02108

ISBN 978-0-9904395-1-6
Library of Congress Number: 2017947890
The Society of King's Chapel

Printed in the United States of America

Dedicated to

Charles Forman
Harriet Parker
Thaxter Spencer
Harry Stokes
Helen Thompson
Elizabeth Thomson
Rudolf Toch
Ned Wight

Members of the
committee that from
1981 to 1986 prepared
the ninth revision of
The Book of Common Prayer
according to the use in
King's Chapel, Boston.

INTRODUCTION

When I retired from my ministry at King's Chapel, a church that worships in a modified Anglican tradition, I wanted to do one more thing for the congregation. I wanted to provide them with an account of the history, faith, and reasoning on which their prayer book and worship are based.

At King's Chapel the congregation is responsible for maintaining prayer book worship. The better they know their tradition, the more they will appreciate it, and the more wisely they will revise that text when the occasion arises. It is for them, my liturgical companions for more than thirty years, that I have been researching, writing, and rewriting this text.

I did not do this alone. Parishioners, colleagues, and two excellent editors have turned my incomplete efforts into the book you hold in your hands.

My family, friends, and many of my Unitarian Universalist colleagues who have known of my absorption in this work, may also find this book of some interest.

Over the years I worked on this text, the more I saw it might also help people in the Episcopal Church with whom we at King's Chapel share a common tradition. Aside from Jeff Lee's *Opening the Prayer Book*, published in 1999, I know of no layperson's guide to prayer book worship in that household of faith aside from a six-page pamphlet now out of print. I hope this book will interest and help congregations and perhaps even clergy in the Episcopal church.

A note on how to read this guide.

I suggest you first read "Why A Book of Common Prayer" and "The History of the Prayer Book." These sections will provide the background that will make sense of all that follows.

You will encounter words you do not know. Find their meaning in the Glossary at the end of this book. If you don't find a definition you need, please let me know.

You may want a Bible at hand, since many biblical passages are designated only by citation. You also might want to refer to a King's Chapel prayer book. If you don't have one, you can order one from admin@kings-chapel.org.

To learn more of the history, people, and events mentioned in this book, you can buy a copy of *The Oxford Dictionary of the Christian Church*, a valuable resource for lay people as well as clergy.

Now I wish you joy in your reading and reflections.

Carl Scovel
Minister Emeritus of King's Chapel, Boston, 2017

Contents

Morning Prayer.

Amen.

¶ *Then shall be read distinctly with an audible voice the First Lesson, taken out of the Old Testament, as is appointed in the Kalendar, (except there be proper Lessons assigned for that day:) He that readeth, so standing, and turning himself, as he may best be heard of all such as are present. And after that, shall be said or sung in English, the Hymn called Te Deum Laudamus, daily throughout the year.*

¶ *Note, That before every Lesson the Minister shall say,* Here beginneth such a Chapter, or Verse of such a Chapter of such a Book *And after every Lesson,* Here endeth the First, or the Second Lesson.

Te Deum Laudamus.

WE praise thee, O God: we acknowledge thee to be the Lord.

All the earth doth worship thee: the Father everlasting.

To thee all Angels cry aloud: the Heavens, and all the Powers therein.

To thee Cherubin, and Seraphin: continually do cry,

Holy, Holy, Holy : Lord God of Sabaoth.

The Father : of an infinite Majesty;

Thine honourable, true and only Son;

Also the Holy Ghost: the Comforter.

Thou art the King of Glory : O ~~Christ.~~ Lord

[handwritten:] Jesus Christ is thy well beloved Son.

[handwritten:] When thou gavest him to Man, it pleased thee that he be born of a Virgin.

[handwritten:] When he had over the Sharpness of Death, the Kingdom of Heaven Believers.

[handwritten:] He sitteth at hand of God, in the G the Father:

[handwritten:] We beli he shall come to be our Ju We therefore pray thee Servants whom thou hast thro his most precious Blo

Make them to be numbered with thy Saints: in Glory everlasting.

O Lord, save thy people and bless thine heritage.

Govern them: and lift them up for ever.

Day by day : we magnifie

A page from an eighteenth-century reprint of the 1662 Anglican
Book of Common Prayer with James Freeman's alterations written in ink.

WHY A BOOK OF COMMON PRAYER?

—————— ✠ ——————

Think of the prayer book as the script of a play. The play is the liturgy. The stage is the church. The plot is a story, neither a farce nor a tragedy, but a comedy—a divine comedy. We, the worshipers, are the cast. And the world, not us, is the audience.

The words in this play are precious. They are holy. They are holy because they tell the story of our life, the true story, the story of our life in God and God's life in us. These words are essential to our well-being, and therefore we enact them in the liturgy.

The Christian play needs a cast and each member of the cast needs the others in order to play his or her unique role in this drama. Our fellow players teach us how to pray, when to pray, where to pray, and why. And when that happens, the play comes alive.

But why a book? A book is tactile. It can be touched and felt. It is easily picked up and laid down. A book is sequential, so one can readily find one's place in it and one's way through it. A book is also easy on the eyes.

Why *common* prayer?

In 1549 when Thomas Cranmer created a prayer book for the Church of England, he did something unprecedented. For the first time in Christian history people and priest held in their hands the same book with all the essential services of the church. The priest became as accountable to the people as they were to him. People and priest became co-celebrants in the church's worship, the great drama of God's redemption.

That is why Cranmer called this a book of common prayer. The clergy were no longer praying for the people but leading the people in their prayers. So it was in 1549, and so it is today.

Why prayer? We pray because we are born with a desire to enter a world that is larger, truer, better, and more beautiful than the world we live in. This desire to be part of something more leads some people to addictions, some to obsessions, some to cults, and some to a quest for power.

It leads others to prayer, connecting us with the unseen center of our being. This center radiates power, wisdom, peace, compassion, healing, and transformation. We name this center in many ways, but most often as God.

We pray, of course, in many ways—by singing, speaking, reading, writing, thinking, meditating, serving others, or playing a lovely sport. When we pray through a prayer book, we join our desires and prayers with those who worship with us now, with those who came before us, and those who will follow. In company with all of these we enter and enact the divine comedy, the great play of our redemption.

**

Within the prayer book stands another and even more important book, namely, the Bible. The Bible is important not just because of the genealogies, hymns, histories, legends, letters, poems, prayers, proverbs, prophecies, and visions that we find in it.

The Bible is important because it is a story, a great story, the story of our humankind. It is a story that begins in a garden and ends in a city, a holy city, the city of God. And this story is the text on which the drama of Christian worship is based.

The biblical story has two main characters—God and humankind. It begins with our birth and innocence. Then comes our fall into discontent, rebellion, hatred, fear, and violence, and, finally, our faltering struggle to become again the people we were made to be.

Just as God spoke us into being, so God continues to speak to us through prophets and sages in our time. In the Christian part of this story, God becomes a human being who lives, dies, and rises for us. He gives us His spirit and the company of His disciples, the church, the cast that we are part of. Together we enact God's promise that God's kingdom will come, now only in part, but someday in its completeness.

We live in the middle of this story, in the fall, forgiveness, renewal, and the promise. Despite our present captivity within a violent history, the Bible tells us that at the end we will find our way into the holy city. We may not see this in our lifetimes, but it will come. When we worship, we can sometimes feel as if the kingdom has already come into our lives.

When Christians worship, they encounter the Bible's story in three ways.

First, at every service they hear readings from the two great covenants God made with humankind, first with the Jews in the Old Testament and then with the Christians in the New. In the sermon that follows these readings, the preacher interprets their meaning to the congregation.

Next, much of the prayer book text comes from the Bible. The psalms and chants that we read or sing, the prayers, the Lord's Prayer, the greetings, and the benedictions are taken or adapted from the Bible.

Finally, the prayers of the prayer book are filled with the great themes of the Bible: creation, fall, sin, judgment, repentance, forgiveness, thanksgiving, praise, compassion, fellowship, justice, peace, and hope.

For example, in Advent we express our longing for God's presence. At Christmas we celebrate God's coming to us. During Lent and at Easter we reflect on what God's coming demands of us, and rediscover our lives in the light of Christ's suffering, crucifixion, and resurrection. During the Pentecost season, the last half of the church year, we consider the many ways God calls us and how we respond. All this constitutes our life in the liturgy, life as a member of a cast called to enact the Bible's story.

Until Gutenberg perfected his printing press in the late fifteenth century, books had been written by hand. Mass production due to the new press made Archbishop Thomas Cranmer's *Book of Common Prayer* available in multiple copies for use by common people, not only by the clergy.

This image, printed in the early 1500s, depicts workers in Jodocus Badius's printing office, the Ascension Press, reprinted by A. F. Butsch in *Die Bücher-Ornamentick Der Renaissance* (vol. ii), published in 1991

THE HISTORY OF THE PRAYER BOOK

———————— ✠ ————————

Two events made possible a book of common prayer—the invention of printing and the reformation of the church. Before those two events the people were spectators at services conducted in Latin by the clergy and largely for the clergy. In order to conduct these daily and Sunday services a parish priest needed at least seven books; cathedral clergy needed more than a dozen. All liturgical books were handwritten, therefore expensive, and hard to come by. In both church and cathedral the congregation held their rosaries in their hands, the Lord's Prayer and Hail Mary in their minds, and their own petitions in their hearts. And so it was for more than a thousand years.

All this changed with inventors like Johannes Gutenberg and preachers like Martin Luther. People began to read the whole Bible in their own tongue instead of hearing snippets of scripture in Latin at the mass. Simultaneously, clergy began to see that worship was the work of the people as well as that of the priest.

These events led to two forms of worship in Reformation churches. The Reformed churches of France, Switzerland, Bohemia, the Netherlands, and Scotland and the churches of the left wing of the Reformation, such as the Anabaptists, Mennonites, and later the Methodists, took one direction. Their worship services consisted of scripture readings, prayers, preaching, and hearty hymn singing. These services survive in Baptist, Methodist, Presbyterian, Disciples, United Church of Christ, and Evangelical churches in our time.

The Lutheran churches in Germany and the Anglican churches in England went in another direction. They took the services they had inherited from the Church of Rome, radically revised and recombined them, and incorporated them into a single book, the Lutheran *Formulae Missae* in Germany and the Anglican *Book of Common Prayer* in England.

The English Reformation had a bumpy beginning. Henry VIII's desire for a male heir, his divorce from Catherine of Aragon, his first wife, and his subsequent marriage to Anne Boleyn led Pope Clement VII to annul both his divorce and second marriage. Henry retaliated by declaring himself head of the Church of England, effectively separating that church from the authority of Rome. The English bishops confirmed his action in 1524.

When the old Archbishop of Canterbury died, Henry appointed Thomas Cranmer, an early supporter of his divorce, to take that position. Cranmer thus became the most powerful man in the English church.

Cranmer, a professor at Cambridge, was a scholar as well as a politician. He knew Latin, Greek, and Hebrew and was familiar with the Catholic liturgical experiments in Spain and Cologne. Through his reading of Calvin, Luther, and Zwingli he knew the Protestant liturgical reforms in Germany and Switzerland. Cranmer had also read the Eastern liturgies in Greek before they were translated into English.

The First *Book of Common Prayer*, 1549

Henry VIII made no immediate changes in the church's services, but his successor, Edward VI, wanted a single liturgy to be used in all English churches, abbeys, and cathedrals. In 1547 he directed Cranmer to prepare a prayer book for such a liturgy. Two years later Cranmer produced a book of common prayer, titled *The First Prayer Book of Edward VI.*

This book contained all the services of public worship to be held in the Church of England, namely, Morning and Evening Prayer (read daily), Holy Communion (to be celebrated every Sunday) and services for holy days (observed annually). The Epistle and Gospel lessons and the collects for Sundays and holy days were printed in full, as were the psalms, which were divided into thirty-one sections, each section to be read on the numbered day of the month.

The new prayer book also contained services for baptism, confirmation, matrimony, the churching of women, the visitation of the sick, the communion of the sick, and burial. All this was the work of Cranmer, who himself wrote, adopted, adapted, or edited the entire contents of the book.

The Second *Book of Common Prayer*, 1552

The first prayer book satisfied neither the Protestant-minded clergy who wanted a complete break from Rome nor the traditionalists who wanted a more modest reform. In 1552, at the behest of the Edward VI, Cranmer took up his pen again and revised the first book.

In this edition he added an act of confession and absolution to Morning Prayer, Evening Prayer, and Holy Communion. In the latter service he rephrased the prayer of consecration stating Christ's "real presence" in broad, ambiguous terms. He added a rubric that made it clear that kneeling at Holy Communion did not imply that the communicant was worshipping the elements (the consecrated bread and wine) but rather that they were worshipping God and Christ.

The new book directed clergy, when leading worship, to wear only a surplice, not the ornate vestments of the past. At the end of the 1552 book, Cranmer added the Thirty-nine Articles, which were the Church of England's requirements for faith and practice.

Upon the publication of the 1552 revision, Parliament passed the Act of Uniformity, which made the services in the prayer book the only services that could be used for public worship in England. The penalty for disobedience was a fine for the first offense, imprisonment for the second, and life imprisonment for the third.

Hardly had this book been published than Edward VI died, and Mary Tudor, a devout Catholic, came to power. During her five years on the throne she restored the old Latin rite, banned prayer book worship, and burned at the stake its unrepentant supporters, including Thomas Cranmer.

When Mary's half-sister, Elizabeth, came to power in 1558, she restored use of the 1552 prayer book. This book, modestly revised in 1662, became the prayer book of all Anglican churches in America, including King's Chapel.

An Anglican Church Becomes Unitarian

No liturgy stands unchanged by what happens around it. Social, intellectual, and financial forces may cause a church either to conform or resist. Such was the case in Boston after the American Revolution.

With the exodus of most Patriot families in Boston during the British occupation and later the departure of Loyalist families with the British army, only twelve families were left in King's Chapel in 1776, and they were without a priest. After worshipping with the Old South congregation for five years, this remnant interviewed a young, unordained Harvard graduate, James Freeman. (For more on Freeman's life see the Key Figures section.)

King's Chapel gave him the title of lay reader and authorized him to read Morning and Evening Prayer as well as to preach and "deliver at other times such sermons as are most approved by you." He was to drop all prayers for the British royalty and government and to read the Athanasian Creed during Holy Communion at his own discretion. Freeman made other changes to the liturgy, as we learn from a letter he wrote his father in Quebec: "I trust you believe that, by entering into this line, I have imbibed no High Church notions ... for the Proprietors of the Chapel ... allow me to make several alterations in the service, which liberty I frequently use."

Despite his low-church inclinations Freeman accepted the call, but within two years he was chafing at certain doctrines in the prayer book. When he expressed his discontent to the Proprietors (the pew holders), they asked him to preach on his beliefs, and this he did in the fall of 1784, expecting that these would be his last sermons at King's Chapel.

To his surprise the Proprietors took his objections seriously and in January of 1785 voted that "some alterations be made in some parts of the Liturgy." They appointed a committee of seven to assist Freeman in this task, and thus the stage was set for the first revision of our prayer book.

Freeman, at heart a simple congregationalist, had no formal education in Christian worship. The Proprietors themselves knew little of theology or liturgy. How then were these two parties to reform a 225-year-old liturgy, a task for which they were ill-prepared and that they might have to defend in court if a bishop or the neighboring Episcopal churches contested King's Chapel's right to their sanctuary?

The answer to this dilemma came in the person of William Hazzlitt, a British émigré and a former member of Theophilus Lindsey's independent congregation in London. Hazzlitt provided Freeman with a copy of Lindsey's reformed Anglican liturgy, which became the model for the changes made at King's Chapel. (For more on this story, see first "Clarke" and then "Lindsey" in the Key Figures section.)

The 1785 Prayer Book

With Hazzlitt's prayer book in hand and in consultation with his committee, Freeman proceeded to write his proposed emendations into a 1728 edition of the 1662 prayer book. During the next three months he and the committee of seven produced a trial prayer book, which, after six weeks of use, won the support of the congregation. At their annual meeting on Easter Monday in 1785, the Proprietors voted on the changes paragraph by paragraph, and approved many, though not all, of Freeman's recommendations.

Freeman and his committee made three kinds of substantial changes.

First, there were theological changes. Prayers formerly addressed to the Son and holy Spirit were now addressed to God the Father. For example, "O God the Son who hast redeemed the world" became "O God, who by thy Son hast redeemed the world." But the Proprietors did not endorse Freeman's preference that all prayers be addressed directly to God, since Jesus specifically told his disciples that whatever they asked the Father in his name would be granted. (John 16:23) Therefore, to this day prayers at King's Chapel are addressed to God "through Jesus Christ."

Trinity Sunday was dropped from the church calendar, and the Sundays once numbered after that day were numbered after Pentecost, or Whitsunday.

In the new prayer book God was referred to as Father, Son, and holy Spirit only when so cited in scripture. Freeman had hoped that these Trinitarian references would be dropped, but the Proprietors held that since they were scriptural, they should stay, and they did. Therefore the benediction from II Corinthians 13:14 concludes several services in the prayer book. Children and adults are baptized in the name of the Father, Son, and holy Spirit as directed by Jesus in Matthew 28:18.

Since the Gloria Patri, "Glory be to the Father and to the Son and to the holy Spirit," does not appear in scripture, Freeman, following Lindsey's precedent, chose a doxology from I Timothy 1:17, which reads, "Now to the King eternal, immortal, invisible, the only wise God, be honor and glory through Jesus Christ forever and ever. Amen." (For more, see Doxology in the Glossary.)

The 1785 book dropped the recitation of the Athanasian Creed from Holy Communion and the 1811 revision dropped the Apostles' Creed from Morning Prayer, although the latter still appears in gold-leaf lettering on one of the panels in the church's chancel.

It is not surprising that King's Chapel, being charged with abandoning the faith of its founders, stopped praying in the litany for deliverance "from all false doctrines, heresy, and schism."

In short, the theology of the new prayer book was distinctly Unitarian. Jesus Christ, though divine in his mission to humanity, was subordinate to God the Father. Freeman supported this position through numerous biblical citations in his introduction to the 1785 revision. To this day the theology of the King's Chapel prayer book is distinctly Unitarian Christian. It is, incidentally, a position also held by Jehovah's Witnesses, some Baptist churches and, probably many other Christians.

A second kind of change made in the 1785 edition was what we might call a more positive view of God, specifically in the use of the psalms. As earlier mentioned, the 1785 prayer book printed the entire Psalter, but put in italics those portions "liable to be misconstrued or misapplied." These verses were those announcing God's wrath against His enemies and praying for their destruction, sometimes in the most violent terms. Such verses, constituting a large portion of the Psalter, were presumably not read aloud.

A third set of changes come from Freeman's and the committee's low church (or congregational) inclinations. In all rubrics "priest" becomes "minister," and "sacrament" becomes "ordinance." The dictionary defines ordinance as "an ordering of events." Since the King's Chapel reformers believed that only God had the power to forgive sins, the minister's pronouncement of absolution became the minister's prayer for forgiveness.

In this low-church view of the 1785 editors, the interpretation of Holy Communion became more "spiritual" than physical. The communion prayer in the 1662 version says, "Grant us so to eat the flesh of thy dear Son Jesus Christ and to drink his blood, that our sinful bodies may be made clean by his body and our souls washed through his most precious blood." The 1785 revision printed in its place, "Grant us, therefore, gracious Lord, so to partake of this holy ordinance, that our minds may be impressed with gratitude to thy dear Son Jesus Christ..."

Other alterations included the addition of a catechism written by Joseph Priestley, (see Key Figures) for the instruction of children and the deletion of "obey" from the bride's vows in the wedding service.

A more detailed description of what followed the publication of this book, including James Freeman's ordination and the subsequent ecclesiastical conflict, may be found in *Journey Toward Independence* by Carl Scovel and Charles Forman, Skinner House, 1993, available at King's Chapel.

The 1811 to 1841 Prayer Books

The next four editions brought to the prayer book an influx of services, prayers, and hymns, which remained there until 1918.

This began with the 1811 edition. Freeman gave his new and short-lived assistant, Samuel Cary, authority to create a second revision. Cary introduced four complete services of Morning and Evening Prayer, which he found in the prayer books of churches in Liverpool and Salisbury, England. These services, formal and biblical, followed the basic structure of Morning and Evening Prayer. The 1811 revision also added many collects and prayers, including one for "malefactors after condemnation."

This same edition dropped "and there is no health in us" from the General Confession, reflecting a more positive view of humankind, an optimism that continued in successive revisions. The 1828 edition dropped "wickedness" from its Eucharistic confession.

Freeman's successor, Francis William Pitt Greenwood, edited the next three editions, 1828, 1831, and 1841. The growing number of children in the parish provided the occasion for adding not only several Sunday school services to the book, but also six services for families to use at home.

Greenwood felt that the inherited service of Evening Prayer, being only a slight variation from Morning Prayer, was "not well calculated to engage the attention of the congregation," and therefore, included a second form of that service.

Greenwood thought the congregation should be singing hymns other than Tate and Brady's metrical settings of the Psalter. This led to the inclusion of a hundred hymns written by Isaac Watts and the Methodist brothers, John and Charles Wesley, as well as some hymns from the Moravian tradition. In explanation he wrote in the introduction, "Their delightful fervor, though by some will be thought to be methodistical, will be thought by others, I trust, to be the true spirit of Christian devotion."

He also saw that the prayer book should be not just a collection of public services, but also in his words, "a manual of devotions as well, to be taken back to the worshipper's house, to go with the traveller on his journey and the sailor on the sea ..." For this reason Greenwood included prayers for personal devotions and occasions.

Greenwood was a high church Unitarian. He restored the Priestley catechism, which had been dropped in the 1811 edition, as well as the phrase, "Thine honorable, true, and only Son and the holy Ghost" to the litany. He defended from excision St. Paul's words for baptism in the name of the Father, Son, and holy Ghost.

Greenwood also deleted forty psalms entire from the Psalter and many verses from other psalms. Duplications in text, references to historical events, pleas to a wrathful God, imprecations against enemies, and exultations over their destruction were all deemed just cause for excision. Subsequent editions omitted or readmitted various psalms.

The authority of Greenwood's final prayer book (1841) was so great that it continued with only slight alterations for almost eighty years. It seems that many of his additions were never used, for Greenwood defended their retention in his introduction to the 1841 book, "not because they are used but because at some time they may be found to be useful."

The 1918 and 1925 Prayer Books

The singular action of the 1918 prayer book was the excision of almost everything that earlier editions had added: the two alternate Sunday services, the church school services, the family services, the Priestley catechism, many prayers, the private devotions, communion for the sick, saints' days, hymns, and even more psalms, so that of the original 150 only thirty-seven were left intact.

All this happened without any explanation other than an enigmatic sentence in the preface stating that every effort had been made "to bring the language of the service into closer agreement with what is taken to be the thought and feeling of enlightened religion today."

The 1918 prayer book made three further excisions: the phrase "miserable offenders" from the confession in Morning Prayer, and from the confession in Holy Communion "provoking most justly thy wrath and indignation" and "the burden of them (our sins) is intolerable." An earlier edition had removed "there is no health in us" from the confession in Morning Prayer.

Since this revised prayer book was printed in a trial book in 1915 and used, presumably, for some time without recorded dissent, these changes seem to have been made with the congregation's consent.

For people seeking "enlightened religion," these excisions must have seemed reasonable. For those of us, however, who have lived through the violence of the last century as well as this one, the confession of our precarious and culpable human condition may be indispensable.

The 1918 prayer book added a short communion service based on Eastern texts and the newly discovered *Didache* (pronounced "deedakay") or *The Teaching of the Twelve Apostles*, a second-century manual of faith and practice. There is no record and no memory of this service ever being used, and it was not kept in the 1986 revision.

The 1925 prayer book, which followed its predecessor by only seven years, made a few small changes, and those were in the communion service. These changes were voted line-by-line and phrase-by-phrase at two long, painful parish meetings. These meetings, remembered and recounted by those who were present, remain a warning on how not to make liturgical decisions.

The Improvisations of Joseph Barth

The ministry of Joseph Barth (1955–1965) shows us how liturgical practice can change without altering a word in the prayer book. Raised a Catholic in Kansas and trained at the University of Chicago, Dr. Barth brought both influences to King's Chapel.

Prior to his arrival, the Sunday service began with the act of confession. Dr. Barth introduced the singing of a hymn as the first act of worship at the Sunday service. He also introduced the procession of the congregation's gifts to the chancel and the singing of "We give Thee but Thine own." He introduced the imposition of ashes on Ash Wednesday and was the first minister to face the congregation from behind the table during Holy Communion. He reinstituted the position of lay reader, which had not been filled since the church's call to James Freeman. He asked Harry Stokes, an unordained graduate of Harvard Divinity School and director of the church school, to assume that role.

He introduced two new services, the *Tenebrae* service on Good Friday evening and the annual welcoming of new members. He made these changes without fanfare and with the implicit consent of the congregation, leaving a significant, though unprinted, legacy.

The 1986 Prayer Book

The 1986 revision included in slightly amended form the traditional services for Morning Prayer, Midday Prayers, Evening Prayer, and Holy Communion, and added Evensong and a second order for Holy Communion. These services are described later in this guide.

The 1986 revision also included the amended or newly-instituted services for Christmas, Good Friday, and Easter Eve as well as orders for the visitation of the sick and welcoming new members. It modified the orders for baptism, matrimony, and burial.

The new King's Chapel prayer book added more than thirty hymns that the congregation had been singing for fifty years even though they were not in the hymnal. Four litanies were included in addition to the *Great Litany* and the *Decalogue*.

A great body of prayers, carefully chosen and sometimes rephrased, were added for personal needs such as rest, health, and comfort, for public concerns such as creation, justice, and homelessness, and for such church events as concerts and parish meetings.

Like Francis Greenwood in 1828, the committee hoped to create a book that would serve as a manual for private prayer as well as for public worship.

Experimentation is an inherent part of liturgical evolution. The 1986 committee considered liturgical changes that other churches had made. They learned from those changes, even when they did not follow their direction.

Thirty years have passed since the publication of the 1986 edition. It has preserved as well as expanded the church's services. In light of current liturgical experimentation it may seem to be a conservative book. If this is true, it was probably the committee's intent. The committee believed that the best change and the most permanent is that which moves deliberately rather than hastily and anxiously.

For example, the committee was divided over the language of gender inclusivity. Clearly, there was a sense that much needed to be done, but there was no great enthusiasm for either a new literalism or for impersonal references to the deity.

The 1986 edition does not include the entire Christmas Eve and Easter Eve services. These services require complex instructions and lengthy texts that vary from year to year. The church now prints separate orders of worship for these services.

Readers should note that a prayer book tradition lives only when it moves. The addition of new services, whether printed in the prayer book or not, gives life to the services inherited from the past. King's Chapel has a history of such services: an annual Thanksgiving Day service in 1898, the *Tenebrae* service in 1955, the Easter Vigil in 1972, a second order for Holy Communion in 1978, and, in 2015, an early Sunday service, "Morning Light," at the Little Chapel, and Holy Communion at King's Chapel on Wednesday evenings. Such additions are indeed part of our tradition.

In time the current prayer book will be supplanted by a tenth edition, whose editors, we hope, will have learned something from our efforts as well as from the congregation's own experience at worship during the lifetime of this, the ninth edition.

Three Women in Church was painted by the German realist,
Wilhelm Leibl (1844-1900), between the years 1878-81 when he
was living in the town of Berbling in Bavaria.

THE PRAYER SERVICES

——————— ✠ ———————

Five features characterize Morning, Midday, and Evening Prayer and Evensong.

They are biblical, based on the words, narrative, and faith found in scripture.

They are historical. They include prayers, chants, psalms, hymns, and litanies that Christians have said and sung for almost twenty centuries. Morning Prayer itself moves through time—from the church's origins in Judaism (The Old Testament readings and chants), through the church's birth (the New Testament readings and chants), and ending with prayers for the church, state, and world in our time.

They are didactic, teaching us how God creates, corrects, forgives, guides, and sustains his people, as well as how our humankind both fails and succeeds in its religious ventures.

They are poetic: metered, metaphoric, and memorable. The rhythms, cadence, and images of these services evoke our imagination, arouse our minds, and help us remember them.

These services are congregational. A specific people in a specific church sing the chants and hymns together. They say the psalms and prayers together. They hear scripture and its interpretation together.

At King's Chapel, because the congregation itself authorizes each new edition at a formal meeting of the parish, it owns its liturgy and is responsible for it.

The Story of Morning and Evening Prayer

Jewish worship began as simple rituals of animal sacrifice, enacted in several holy places. By the end of his reign, King David had made the temple in Jerusalem the sole center for these rituals. By then the sacrifices were more formal and elaborate, enhanced with chants, drums, trumpets, and ornately-vested priests who circled the main altar, which was wreathed with fire and smoke and ran with the blood of its slaughtered victims.

In 585 BCE, Nebuchadnezzar captured Jerusalem, destroyed its walls and temple, and carried Israel's kings, princes, priests, and their families and retinue to Babylon. Thus ended the magnificent rituals in Jerusalem's temple.

Deprived of these rituals, the exiled Jews in Babylon met in small groups to pray and study their scripture, the Torah. In Babylon they learned to sing the Lord's song in a strange land and how to survive as a people. In doing so, they began a tradition that lives today.

In time many exiles came to feel at home in Babylon so that when their new ruler, Cyrus of Persia, gave them a chance to return to Jerusalem, they chose to stay. By staying in Babylon these Jews made Babylon a center of Jewish learning, second only to Jerusalem

Other Jews, however, returned to their desolate homeland. The book of Nehemiah describes how they rebuilt the walls of Jerusalem and a new, if less glorious, temple. There they resumed the tradition of morning and evening sacrifices.

Many of the returning exiles did not stay in Jerusalem, but moved to towns and villages throughout the province of Judea. Morning and evening, when the priests in the temple in Jerusalem were offering sacrifices, these local congregations in Judea gathered to pray, study, and sing the psalms as they had in Babylon. They met in buildings called in Greek a synagogue (literally, a meetinghouse). In the Nazareth meetinghouse Jesus learned the psalms, prayers, and scriptures of his people.

Jesus was a Jew, as were most of the first Christians. Therefore, for at least two decades they continued to meet and pray in synagogues. Those early Christians antagonized most Jews, who were still waiting for their long-delayed Messiah, by proclaiming that he had already arrived in Jesus of Nazareth. Since, under Syria, Greece, and Egypt, Jews had endured captivity for several centuries and still bowed under the Roman yoke, the Christian claim was an offense to their common sense and denied their suffering.

The unconventional Jews who followed Jesus soon acquired a new name, Christian, meaning "someone belonging to Christ." This name was first used in Antioch (Acts 11:26), possibly to distinguish them from traditional Jews.

These first Christians continued to meet morning and evening and to pray, read the psalms, and hear scriptures, as they had as Jews. But they also read the letters of St. Paul and the first Gospels, and they celebrated the presence of their Christian Messiah in a service they called the Eucharist (Greek for "the thanksgiving"), the service we call Holy Communion.

St. Paul's letters testify that these first Christians experienced new life in Jesus the Christ. This life enabled them to face not only exclusion, hostility, and persecution from without, but division, confusion, and faithlessness from within. Both Paul's letters and those of the first bishops make it clear that the young church was no gathering of saints. Yet the church survived and grew.

By 325 CE the church of the persecuted was becoming the church of the empire. Christians began to enjoy the power and privileges that once supported the cult of the emperor and other pagan religions.

Some Christians, grieved at the church's expanding wealth and power, convinced of its corruption, and despairing of its reform, left the cities where Christianity flourished. These men and women went to the deserts of Syria, Palestine, and the Nile delta, where they founded small communities devoted to silence, solitude, and prayer.

These fathers and mothers of the desert fed themselves from their gardens and made money for other necessities by selling baskets that they wove. At times, they left their huts to pray together. These gatherings for common prayer became daily services, called "offices," following the injunction in Psalm 119:164: "Seven times a day do I praise thee."

In time these offices included three morning services (matins, lauds, and prime) and two evening services (vespers before supper and compline before retiring). These five services plus two or three at midday (according to local practice) became their daily worship. To this day these services are said and sung in abbeys and cathedrals.

As we noted earlier, Henry VIII repudiated the authority of the pope, made himself head of the Church of England and chose Thomas Cranmer, Archbishop of Canterbury, to lead the revision of the liturgies inherited from Rome.

In the first *Book of Common Prayer*, published in 1549, Cranmer and his bishops combined the monastic offices of matins, lauds, and prime into a single service that was Morning Prayer. He combined vespers and compline into Evening Prayer. He directed that these services be read seven days of the week by the local priest and congregation in every church in England and also that Holy Communion be celebrated every Sunday.

English congregations did not obey this last directive and for good reason. As Catholics they had received communion only once a year, the custom for more than a thousand years. Instead of communing, they simply looked up from their private prayers as the host (the sacramental bread) and the cup (the sacramental wine) was lifted up by the celebrant. On most Sundays, observing the mystery was considered sufficient for the laity. Once a year at the most, and usually on Easter Sunday, the laity received the host, but not the cup, which was reserved for the clergy. Given this millennial-long precedent, it wasn't likely that the English laity were going to take communion every week.

Thus, Morning Prayer became the usual Sunday morning service in most Anglican churches. In the late 1800s the priests in the Oxford Movement initiated a liturgical reform that made Holy Communion the central Sunday celebration. By the 1960s in this country Holy Communion had became the normative Sunday service, though some Episcopal churches still hold Morning Prayer on Sunday mornings. King's Chapel and perhaps a few Episcopal churches remain what are called "Morning Prayer churches," holding communion only on the first Sunday of the month.

Morning Prayer
(Pages 1 – 18 in the prayer book)

Morning Prayer takes us on a spiritual journey of five stages. The journey begins with confession, that is, the General Confession, a thoughtful acknowledgment made before God and our neighbors of our failings and fallen condition. This is followed by the minister's assurance of forgiveness.

In the Episcopal and Catholic traditions the priest pronounces God's forgiveness. We then say the Lord's Prayer, which reminds us that to be forgiven we must also forgive; otherwise we are not ready to receive God's forgiveness.

The second stage is praise, when we honor God by singing a chant, reading a psalm, and singing a doxology.

The third stage is instruction. We hear a lesson, first from the Old Testament and then from the New. After each reading we sing a chant.

At the fourth stage we pray for ourselves (the first three collects), then for the world (all nations), then the church (clergy and people), and finally for all sorts and conditions of our humankind.

Fifth and finally, we thank God for life, our blessings, and the promise of our completion through Christ in the words of the General Thanksgiving.

These five stages are actually listed in the Exhortation to Confession at the beginning of Morning Prayer, namely: 1. Confession – "… humbly to acknowledge our sins before God," 2. Praise – "… to set forth his most worthy praise," 3. Instruction – "… to hear his most holy word," 4. Petition – "… to ask those things which are requisite and necessary for the body as for the soul," and 5. Thanksgiving – "… to render thanks for the great benefits which we have received at his hands."

Presently the congregation at King's Chapel opens its Sunday worship by singing a hymn, the practice begun in 1955 by its then-new minister, the Rev. Joseph Barth. The 1986 revision formalized this practice with the following rubric: "All shall stand and sing the Introit."

On most Sundays, the minister invites the congregation to read two or three Bible verses and then the Exhortation. On the last Sunday of the month, when the Great Litany is read, the minister reads the shorter invitation to confession in place of the following Exhortation.

Dearly beloved, the Scripture moveth us in sundry places to acknowledge and confess our manifold sins and wickedness, and that we should not dissemble nor cloak them before the face of almighty God our heavenly Father; but confess them with a humble, lowly, penitent, and obedient heart; to the end that we may obtain forgiveness of the same, by his infinite goodness and mercy. And although we ought, at all times, humbly to

> acknowledge our sins before God, yet ought we chiefly so to do
> when we assemble and meet together, to render thanks for the
> great benefits that we have received at his hands, to set forth his
> most worthy praise, to hear his most holy word, and to ask those
> things which are requisite and necessary, as well for the body as
> the soul. Wherefore I pray and beseech you, as many as are here
> present, to accompany me, with a pure heart and humble voice,
> unto the throne of the heavenly grace, saying with me:

Such devout words and the very act of confession may seem strange to us who live in a litigious and self-justifying age. It may be hard for us to feel the deep sense of crisis that occasions such a prayer. For at the heart of this prayer lies the conviction that we and all humankind suffer more than we know and stand in serious danger because of what we and others have done and left undone. Our sins are personal and collective, deliberate and thoughtless, voluntary and involuntary. This is the inevitable consequence of our inherent self-centeredness, which is danger-ous in our personal convictions, but far more dangerous in our collective convictions.

The General Confession, which follows, acknowledges this condition.

> Almighty and most merciful Father, we have erred and strayed
> from thy ways like lost sheep. We have followed too much the
> devices and desires of our own hearts. We have offended against
> thy holy laws. We have left undone those things which we ought
> to have done; and we have done those things which we ought
> not to have done. But thou, O Lord, have mercy upon us. Spare
> thou those, O God, who confess their faults. Restore thou those
> who are penitent, according to thy promises declared unto
> mankind in Christ Jesus our Lord. And grant, O most merciful
> Father, that we may hereafter live a godly, righteous, and sober
> life; to the glory of thy holy name. *Amen.*

King's Chapel has a curious history of softening the seriousness of its confessions. The 1811 edition dropped "and there is no health in us." The 1828 edition dropped "wickedness" from its Eucharistic confession. The

1918 prayer book dropped "miserable offenders" from Morning Prayer, and from Holy Communion "provoking most justly thy wrath and indignation against us." In the same service the authors also dropped the phrase, "the burden of them [our sins] is intolerable," reflecting, perhaps accurately, the mindset of an affluent and "enlightened" congregation.

These amendments come from a misunderstanding of both sin and confession. As clients in therapy or members of Alcoholics Anonymous know, the result of confessing and taking responsibility for our misdeeds is not paralysis, but freedom—the freedom to make amends. We approach God, not as the righteous Pharisee, but as the self-searching publican. No one is guiltless, and no one is hopeless. Every saint has a past, and every sinner has a future. With God's help we find the freedom to begin again, and again, and again.

Thomas Cranmer wrote this confession for the service of Morning Prayer. It is a fabric of such biblical phrases as the following: "All we like sheep have gone astray." (Isaiah 53:6); "There is no health in my bones because of my sin."(Psalms 38:3); "God, be merciful to me a sinner." (Luke 18:13); "Have mercy on me, O God, according to thy loving kindness . . . Wash me thoroughly from my iniquity and cleanse me from my sin." (Psalms 51:1-2); ". . . your sins are forgiven for His name's sake." (I John 2:12); "...live sober, upright and godly lives." (Titus 2:12)

Now the minister reads one of the following two prayers, or the assurance of pardon:

> Almighty God, the Father of our Lord Jesus Christ, who desirest not the death of sinners, but rather that they should turn from their wickedness and live: we beseech thee to grant us true repentance, and thy holy Spirit; that those things may please thee which we do at this present, and that the rest of our life hereafter may be pure and holy; so that at the last we may come to thine eternal joy, through Jesus Christ our Lord. *Amen.*

Or this:

> O Lord, we beseech thee mercifully hear our prayers, and spare all those who confess their sins unto thee; that they whose

consciences by sin are accused, by thy merciful pardon may be absolved, through Jesus Christ our Lord. *Amen.*

Or this:

Hear the words of God's promise: "If we confess our sins, God is faithful and just to forgive us our sins and to cleanse us from all unrighteousness." Therefore, let us take heart. God will have mercy upon us, being penitent, pardon and deliver us from all our sins, confirm and strengthen us in all goodness, and bring us to everlasting life.

In the Anglican and Episcopalian services the priest pronounces an absolution and remission of the congregation's sins, based on Jesus' words in John 20:22-23. In the 1786 King's Chapel prayer book, James Freeman, who doubted the priest's power to absolve, made this pronouncement a second prayer for forgiveness said by the minister.

This prayer, like so many in the prayer book, ends with the phrase "through Jesus Christ our Lord." This familiar phrase is derived from John 14:13-14 in which Jesus says, "Whatever you ask in my name that I will do." We must remember that to speak a person's name was to bring them into one's presence.

But what does this mean about Jesus? Who is he in this usage? One may see Jesus as mediator between God and ourselves. One may see him as the one in whose presence we know God. One may see Jesus as God's word made real as one of our human kind. However articulated, Christian faith is based on the collective conviction that God is present in Jesus the Christ, who is both of God and one of us, and therefore the bridge between God and us.

At this point, we say the Lord's Prayer. Like the General Confession it is a "we" prayer, not an "I" prayer. It is found in Matthew 6:6-14 and Luke 11:2-4. In Luke, Jesus teaches a short form (without a concluding doxology), to be repeated word for word by his followers. In Matthew Jesus tells his disciples to pray, not in these words, but in this way. The prayer is not a mantra, but a template. By custom, though, it has become the one prayer most Christians know and say together.

Through this prayer we pray first for the coming of God's kingdom, then for ourselves, and for sustenance, forgiveness, and protection against the evils of this world. In Matthew's version we end with a doxology, which affirms that God is in charge.

Jesus prayed to God as "Our Father" (in Hebrew, *Abinu*) every morning when he said the Eighteen Benedictions in his local synagogue.

The second-century manual of Christian prayer, the *Didache*, tells its readers in chapter 8:7 to say the Matthew version of this prayer three times a day.

In Orthodox churches the congregations may say the Lord's Prayer several times during a service; however, only the priest says the doxology at the end. At King's Chapel, as in most Protestant churches, the congregation says the entire prayer only once during a service.

Christians say this prayer not just at Sunday services and as a private devotion, but also at baptisms, burials, weddings, deathbeds and morning devotions. The Lord's Prayer is, therefore, the "daily bread" of all Christians.

***

The act of praise comes next. Only if one has been astounded by the fact that we exist, that "lifted from the no of all nothing" (e. e. cummings's phrase), we move, breathe, see, hear, labor, love, suffer, struggle, and, by a miracle we call "natural," have landed on this blue-green globe. Only if one has been stunned by such a realization does it make sense to praise anything or Anyone—Person, Presence, Mystery, or Benevolence beyond our understanding, but not beyond the reach of our gratitude.

Such a realization has moved humanity to praise the source of our being, as Jews, Christians, Muslims, Hindus, and many others do with or without a tradition.

At this point in the service, having acknowledged in the Confession that we are not God, we are ready to praise God, beginning with the following versicles based on Psalms 51:15.

Minister O Lord, open thou our lips;
People And our mouth shall show forth thy praise.

These versicles first appeared in *The Apostolic Tradition*, a third-century collection of prayers and services edited by Hippolytus, a Roman priest and theologian. Christian congregations and clergy have greeted each other with these versicles for more than eighteen hundred years,

Minister Now unto the King eternal, immortal, invisible,
          the only wise God;

People   Be honor and glory, through Jesus Christ,
          for ever and ever. *Amen. (I Timothy 1:17; Romans 16:27)*

Minister Praise ye the Lord.

People   The Lord's name be praised.

A doxology is a short act of praise that may be repeated throughout the service. The authoritative Christian doxology is the Gloria Patri: "Glory be to the Father and to the Son and to the holy Spirit; as it was in the beginning, is now and ever shall be, world without end. Amen." Phrases of this doxology are found in Ephesians 3:21, II Peter 3:18, and Jude 1:25, but it did not take its present form until 325 CE when the Council of Nicea defined the classic doctrine of the Trinity.

James Freeman explained his decision not to include the Gloria Patri, by saying that he preferred doxologies from "the pure word of God," namely scripture. He adapted our church's present doxology from that in an English prayer book compiled by the Rev. Theophilus Lindsey for his independent Christian church in London. It reads, "To the king of ages, immortal, invisible, the only wise (meaning "the only") God, be honor and glory forever."

Having said or sung the doxology, at this point we continue our praise by singing one of two chants on alternate Sundays.

The first chant, the *Venite* (the Latin imperative for "come") combines the first seven verses of Psalm 95 with verses 9 and 13 of Psalm 96. The first Anglican prayer books printed all of Psalm 95, including the last four verses, which record God's curse on the Hebrew tribe in the desert, that is, "Therefore I swore in my wrath that they should not enter into my rest." The first American Episcopalian prayer book (1789) dropped these last four verses and added the present verses from Psalm 96. The 1811 edition of our prayer book followed suit.

The second chant, the *Cantate Domino*, "Sing to the Lord," is Psalm 98. The first Christians sang this psalm to Jewish melodies. Later Christians sang this and other chants in plainsong, polyphony, Anglican chant, and hymns in versified texts written by such notables as Martin Luther and Isaac Watts. Cranmer placed this psalm in Morning Prayer, and the 1785 King's Chapel prayer book did the same.

After the chant the congregation and minister read a psalm either in unison or responsively. The 150 psalms are divided into 31 sections, the maximum number of days in a month. Psalms are read in that section whose number corresponds to the date of the month on which the service takes place. At the end of the psalm, congregation and choir sing the doxology they read earlier in the service.

***

We have knelt or bowed for confession. We have stood for praise. Now we sit for instruction.

Let us remember that the ancestor of Morning Prayer is the synagogue service that began in Babylon and was continued by the exiles who returned to Israel. When the young Jesus went to prayers at the Nazareth meetinghouse (synagogue), he would have heard a reading from the Torah and another from the Prophets. The first Christians probably also read two portions of scripture, one from the Torah or Prophets, and the other from one of the Gospels and/or the letters of St. Paul.

Notice that Christian congregations always read an Old Testament lesson. This has not always been the practice. In the first few centuries some Gnostic Christians banned Old Testament readings from their services, claiming they had no relevance for Christians. Most Christian bishops rejected the Gnostic arguments. They maintained that God spoke through the Torah, Prophets, and Writings, as well as through the Gospels and Epistles. The bishops prevailed, but this Gnostic heresy reappeared in Germany in the 1930s when Nazi Christians called on pastors to stop reading from the Jewish scriptures. Again most Christian pastors rejected this call.

Notice that we call the two portions of scripture the Old and the New Testaments. The first Christians called them "the old and new covenant."

St. Jerome translated the Greek word for covenant, *diatheke*, into the Latin *testamentum* (meaning a bequest). The Latin *testamentum* became testament in English translations. "Testament," in current usage, however, rarely means "covenant," but more often evidence, belief, or a will.

Some churches now call the Old Testament the "Hebrew Scriptures," in deference to their Jewish sisters and brothers. Calling these texts "Hebrew" in a Christian context makes them sound like someone else's scriptures, rather than a scripture that Jews and Christians share. It would make no sense to call the New Testament "the Greek scriptures" because in neither case is the language of the original the most significant thing about it. Furthermore, it is no more pejorative to call something old than it is laudatory to call something new.

The church considers the New Testament to be an extension of the Old. However, the New Testament directs Christian faith, worship, practices, and conduct.

Like the Jews in the time of Jesus, having heard instruction from scripture, we thank God for the gift of His Word by singing a chant. On a given Sunday one of the following chants from the Old Testament is sung at the end of the Old Testament reading. *Benedicite* means the imperative of "bless."

O all ye works of the Lord, bless ye the Lord;
  Praise him and magnify him forever.
O ye angels of the Lord, bless ye the Lord;
  O all ye powers of the Lord, bless ye the Lord.
O ye sun and moon, bless ye the Lord;
  O ye showers and dew, bless ye the Lord.
O ye fire and heat, bless ye the Lord;
  O ye dews and frosts, bless ye the Lord.
O ye ice and snow, bless ye the Lord;
  O ye light and darkness, bless ye the Lord.
O let the earth bless the Lord;
  O all ye green things upon the earth, bless ye the Lord.
O all ye fowls of the air, bless ye the Lord;
  O ye children of men, bless ye the Lord.
O ye priests of the Lord, bless ye the Lord;
  O ye spirits and souls of the righteous, bless ye the Lord.

O all ye works of the Lord, bless ye the Lord;
  Praise him and magnify him forever.

Or this:

O all ye works of the Lord, bless ye the Lord;
  Praise him and magnify him forever.
O ye heavens, bless ye the Lord;
  O ye waters that be above the firmament, bless ye the Lord.
O ye stars of heaven, bless ye the Lord;
  O ye winds of God, bless ye the Lord.
O ye winter and summer, bless ye the Lord;
  O ye frost and cold, bless ye the Lord.
O ye nights and days, bless ye the Lord;
  O ye lightnings and clouds, bless ye the Lord.
O ye mountains and hills, bless ye the Lord;
  O ye wells, bless ye the Lord.
O ye seas and floods, bless ye the Lord;
  O ye whales and all that move in the waters, bless ye the Lord.
O all ye beasts and cattle, bless ye the Lord;
  O let Israel bless the Lord.
O ye servants of the Lord, bless ye the Lord;
  O ye holy and humble of heart, bless ye the Lord.
O all ye works of the Lord, bless ye the Lord;
  Praise him and magnify him forever.

The first and second chants, *Benedicite* 1 and 2, are part of a single poem written by a Jew in Alexandria as a late insertion into the story of Shadrach, Meshach, and Abednego. (Daniel 3:1-24) This chapter describes how Nebuchadnezzar ordered three young Jews who refused to worship his image to be thrown into a burning, fiery furnace. When this was done, the king was astonished to see the three walking unhurt among the flames. This unknown author wrote the *Benedicite* as the hymn the three men sang to God as they walked around in midst of the furnace. The text of this song is variously titled "The Song of the Three Holy Children," or "The Three Young Men" or "The Three Jews."

Although the story is set during the reign of Nebuchadnezzar, it was written much later. By telling this story as something that happened four centuries earlier the author was actually praising the Jews of his own time who resisted the persecution of the Seleucid emperor, Antiochus Epiphanes, who reigned from 175-163 BCE.

This chant is an expansion of Psalm 148. Like its original it commands the four orders of creation to praise God for their creation. The first order includes the cosmic powers: angels, sky, sun, moon, stars, waters, winds, rain, dew, frost, ice, snow, light, darkness, lightning, and clouds. The second order of creation includes the earthly powers: green things, mountains, hills, wells, seas, floods, winter, summer, nights, and days. The third order includes the earthly creatures: fowls, beasts, cattle, whales, and everything that moves in the sea. Finally come God's people: humankind, priests, servants, the humble, the holy, and the spirits and souls of the righteous.

Beginning in the fourth century, Christians sang this chant at the early morning office of lauds. Cranmer included it in the 1549 *Book of Common Prayer*. The 1986 King's Chapel prayer book divided this 31-verse chant into two parts, each part with verses that praise God for the four orders of creation.

The third chant that may be sung after the Old Testament reading is Psalm 67, the *Deus Misereatur* (God be merciful), a psalm that ends with prayers for the coming harvest.

The fourth chant that may be sung after the Old Testament reading is Psalm 100, titled *Jubilate Deo*. This chant, meaning "O be joyful in the Lord," was originally sung by the pilgrims who filled the courtyard of the Jerusalem temple for the morning and evening sacrifices. For many centuries Christian monks have chanted this in plainsong at a morning office. In the 1552 *Book of Common Prayer*, Thomas Cranmer directed that it be sung in Morning Prayer.

The next part of instruction is the New Testament lesson. Christians see the two testaments as one story, with the New Testament growing out of the Old. The New Testament is filled with quotations from the psalms and prophets and with allusions to Old Testament figures and stories. Furthermore, Christians see Jesus Christ as the one who has brought to this world the kingdom that the Old Testament prophets foretold.

Tertullian (155 – 240 CE) put it aptly: "Jesus Christ is the kingdom of God in person."

The New Testament is therefore the written witness of the first Christians' experience that in Jesus of Nazareth, God's will and word came as a human being into our confused and strife-torn world. In this figure they found the peace, purpose, and joy that is life in God's kingdom.

The New Testament lesson may be taken from the Gospels, the Epistles or that fascinating book entitled the Revelation to John.

Again we follow the scripture reading with the *Te Deum Laudamus*, meaning "we praise thee, O God."

> We praise thee, O God; we acknowledge thee to be the Lord.
> All the earth doth worship thee, the Father everlasting.
> To thee all angels cry aloud, the heavens and all the
> powers therein.
> To thee cherubim and seraphim continually do cry,
> Holy, holy, holy, Lord God of Sabaoth.
> Heaven and earth are full of the majesty of thy glory.
> The glorious company of the apostles praise thee.
> The goodly fellowship of the prophets praise thee.
> The noble army of martyrs praise thee.
> The holy Church throughout all the world doth
> acknowledge thee,
> The Father of an infinite majesty; thine honorable, true,
> and holy Son;
> Also the holy Ghost, the comforter.
> Thou art the King of glory, O Lord;
> And Jesus Christ is thy well-beloved Son.
> O Lord, save thy people, and bless thine heritage.
> Govern them, and lift them up for ever.
> Day by day we magnify thee;
> And we worship thy Name ever, world without end.
> Vouchsafe, O Lord, to keep us this day without sin.
> O Lord, have mercy upon us; have mercy upon us.
> O Lord, let thy mercy lighten upon us, as our trust is in thee.
> O Lord, in thee have we trusted; let us never be confounded.

Written in the fourth century, after the emperor Constantine established the first pro-Christian government, the *Te Deum* (meaning "To Thee, O God") is attributed to Bishop Nicetus (c. 335-414) of Remesiana (Bela Palanka or Nis in present-day Serbia.) The earliest text of this chant was found in an Irish abbey in Bangor, and was called "A Hymn on the Lord's Day." It may be our oldest non-biblical chant.

The phrase, "Holy, holy, holy" comes from Isaiah's account of his vision in the Jerusalem temple. (Isaiah 6:1-8) The word "holy" in Hebrew is *kadosh*. It means "that which is set apart," namely for the praise and service of God. This reminds us that what we do or say in praise of God are words and actions that set us apart from our daily life, and thus remind us of the transcendent God who says in Isaiah, "My ways are not your ways, nor are my thoughts your thoughts."

In place of the lines in the Anglican prayer book, "Thou art the king of glory, O Christ. Thou art the everlasting Son of the Father," the 1785 King's Chapel prayer book printed, "Thou art the king of glory, O Lord, and Jesus Christ is thy well-beloved Son." Later King's Chapel editions eliminated the next six lines, which speak of the virgin birth, Christ the judge, and even Christ as Savior.

The second of the three New Testament chants, the *Benedictus*, is found in Luke 1:67-79. It is one of four songs found in his account of Christ's birth. In Luke 1:5-25 and 57-66 we read that the angel Gabriel tells Zechariah, a priest in the Jerusalem temple, that his elderly wife, Anna, will bear a son. This son will speak with the spirit of Elijah and should be named John. When Zechariah doubts Gabriel, the angel strikes him dumb. Anna gives birth to a son and names him John. Zechariah regains his voice to affirm his wife's decision and then sings this song of praise. It was sung at lauds in the medieval church and incorporated into Morning Prayer by Cranmer in the 1549 prayer book.

The third chant to be sung after a New Testament reading is the *Magnificat* (meaning "magnify") based on Luke 1:46-55. In this song, Mary, young and pregnant, proclaims God's dismissal of the rich and powerful and God's raising up of the lowly. Her song is derived from the one that the aged Hannah sang after giving birth to the prophet Samuel. (I Samuel 2:1-10)

Beginning in the fourth century, the *Magnificat* was first sung at morning services. But Benedict of Nursia (c. 480-550), who founded the

Benedictine order and wrote its Rule, directed that the *Magnificat* be sung at the evening service in all his abbeys. So it is done to this day in almost all monastic orders.

Cranmer directed that it be sung or recited between the Old and New Testament lessons at Evening Prayer in the 1549 *Book of Common Prayer.* The King's Chapel prayer books followed this precedent until 1986 by which time Evening Prayer was rarely read. The 1986 committee felt that so fine a chant should be sung and heard more often and so placed it in the order for Morning Prayer.

***

We have confessed to God, praised God, and been taught by God's holy word. Now we are ready to pray, or in the words of the exhortation, "to ask those things which are requisite and necessary as well for the body as the soul." Whether we realize it or not, we make two assumptions in so doing.

First, we believe that God will answer our prayer "as may be most expedient for us." That means if we didn't get the bicycle we prayed for at age seven, the honors we hoped for in high school, or the promotion in later years, God gave us the chance to become wiser, tougher, and more real, if we were willing to use the opportunity to do so. In other words, whatever the world gives us, God gives us the power to deal with that.

Second, we assume that praying with our peers in the pews gives us a common kinship with God and a special relationship with those who pray with us. When we pray with people, we know them in a special way.

The clergy lead the people into prayer with an ancient greeting, through which we recognize God's presence in each other:

Minister   The Lord be with you. [Ruth 2:4]
People   And with thy spirit.
Minister   Let us pray. O Lord, show thy mercy upon us;
People   And grant us thy salvation. [Psalm 85:7]
Minister   O God, make clean our hearts within us;
People   And take not thy holy Spirit from us. [Psalm 51:10a, 11b]

We begin by praying for ourselves. These first three prayers are called collects. A collect is a short prayer usually with five parts, namely: a title by which we address God, an ascription by which we understand God, a petition for what we need, a statement of what we hope from that petition and a concluding phrase.

The first prayer, the Collect for Grace, is a good example of this structure: Title – "O God," Ascription – "our heavenly father who hast brought us safely to the beginning of this day," Petition – "defend us in the same by thy mighty power," Desired Outcome – "that we may perfectly love thee and worthily magnify thy holy name," Conclusion – "through Jesus Christ our Lord. Amen."

> O Lord, our heavenly Father, almighty and everlasting God,
> who hast safely brought us to the beginning of this day; defend
> us in the same with thy mighty power; and grant that this day
> we fall into no sin, neither run into any kind of danger; but that
> all our doings may be ordered by thy governance, to do always
> that which is righteous in thy sight, through Jesus Christ our
> Lord. *Amen.*

One of our oldest prayers, it may be based on an even older Jewish prayer, the *Shehecheyanu*: "Blessed art thou, O Lord our God, King of the Universe, who hast kept us, and preserved us, and brought us to this day." Cranmer put this prayer in the 1549 prayer book. Once said only by the minister, since 1986 the congregation now says it with the minister.

The second prayer is the Collect for the Day, so-called because each Sunday in the church year has a specific prayer assigned to it. These prayers, plus sometimes certain chants or Bible verses, are called "propers" because they are specific or proper to a particular Sunday or holy day.

The third prayer, the Collect for Peace, first appeared in a collection of prayers in 400 CE. It was sung at a morning service in Salisbury Cathedral as early as 1300. An earlier version of it reads: "... whom to know is to live forever and whom to serve is to be free."

> O God, who art the author of peace, and lover of concord, in
> knowledge of whom standeth our eternal life, whose service is

perfect freedom; defend us thy humble servants in all assaults of
our enemies, that we, surely trusting in thy defense, may not
fear the power of any adversaries, through Jesus Christ our
Lord. *Amen.*

When we pray for protection from our enemies, we think not only of
individual antagonists, but also collective enemies, such as ideologies,
governments, corporations, causes, and those powers that can corrupt and
harm us. St. Paul called these "principalities and powers." (Romans 8:38,
Ephesians 6:12) When we speak of enemies, we dare not forget the subtle
and unseen enemies within each one of us.

On the last Sunday of the month at King's Chapel, we read the Great
Litany in place of the next five prayers. Commentary about it may be
found in the litany section.

The members of the 1986 committee realized the impact that other
nations can have on our nation and on each other. They concluded that
it was important to pray for all leaders and all peoples, hence the
following prayer:

Almighty God, in whose hand are all the nations of the earth
and from whom all thoughts of love and peace proceed, kindle
in the hearts of all thy people the love of peace; guide those
who govern the nations, that we may receive thy kingdom and
that this earth may be filled with the knowledge of thy love; and
this we ask through him who was called the Prince of Peace,
even Jesus Christ our Lord. *Amen.*

Next we pray for those in authority in our own country.

O Lord, our heavenly Father, high and mighty, King of kings,
Lord of lords, who dost from thy throne behold all the dwellers
upon the earth; most heartily we beseech thee with thy favor to
behold the President, the Congress, and the courts of the
United States, and so replenish them with the grace of thy holy
Spirit, that they may always incline to thy will, and walk in thy
way. Endue them plenteously with heavenly gifts, that in all

their deliberations they may be enabled to promote the national prosperity, and to secure the peace, liberty, and safety of the United States throughout all generations. This we humbly ask in the name of Jesus Christ our Lord. *Amen.*

The first lines of this prayer, based on II Chronicles 20:6 and Psalms 113:5-6 and 33:13-14, affirm that God's power transcends the power of kings, premiers, presidents, chief executive officers, bishops, clergy—in other words, all those in authority. Because the faith of the church rests upon this supra-political claim, the church always stands as a potential threat to the state as well as to all those powers that govern any human institution, including the church itself.

Yet Christians have prayed for civil authorities from earliest times. I Timothy 2:1-2 says, "I urge that supplications, prayers, intercessions, and thanksgivings be made for all people, for kings and all who are in high positions, that we may lead a quiet and peaceable life, godly and respectable in every way." Regardless of our political convictions, we pray for those in power, knowing how their decisions affect us all.

This was originally a prayer for the king, but after our country achieved independence, it became a prayer for the president "and all others in authority." Reflecting a changed political ethos, the 1986 prayer book added "the courts of the United States," but the committee was not ready to include the governor of our commonwealth or the mayor of our city. Presently, however, the ministers at King's Chapel pray for these officials.

Now we pray for all Christian leaders and congregations in words that first appeared in a collection of prayers compiled during the reign of Pope Gelasius (492 – 496) and adopted by Thomas Cranmer for the 1549 prayer book. It is one of the few that have remained unchanged in the King's Chapel prayer book since its inception in 1785.

Almighty and everlasting God, from whom cometh every good and perfect gift; send down upon all ministers of the Gospel, and upon the congregations committed to their charge, the healthful spirit of thy grace; and, that they may truly please thee, pour upon them the continual dew of thy blessing. Grant this, O heavenly Father, for thine infinite mercy's sake in Jesus Christ our Lord. *Amen.*

The 1986 prayer book committee could not agree on replacing all occurrences of the male generic with more inclusive words or phrases. So in the following prayer, and in some other instances, they left the male generic unrevised. Today's ministers may modify this wording when they feel it appropriate.

> O God, the creator and preserver of all mankind, we humbly beseech thee for all sorts and conditions of thy people, that thou wouldst be pleased to make thy ways known unto them, thy saving health unto all nations. More especially we pray for the good estate of thy holy Church; that it may be so guided and governed by thy good Spirit, that all who profess and call themselves Christians

and here the minister sometimes adds "and those who seek Thee by whatever name"

> may be led into the way of truth, and hold the faith in unity of spirit, in the bond of peace, and in righteousness of life. Finally, we commend to thy fatherly goodness all those who are in any way afflicted or distressed in mind, body, or estate, [and especially thy servants . . .]

Here the minister will speak the names of those for whom prayer has been requested:

and those whom we hold up to thee in silent prayer...

At this point the reader pauses.

> May it please thee to comfort and relieve them according to their several necessities; giving them patience under their sufferings, and a happy issue out of all their afflictions; and this we humbly ask as disciples of Jesus Christ our Lord. *Amen.*

Having asked God for those gifts that are "as necessary as well for the body as the soul," the people now thank God for all they have received in the words of the General Thanksgiving.

> Almighty God, Father of all mercies, we thine unworthy ser-
> vants do give thee most humble and hearty thanks for all thy
> goodness and lovingkindness to us and to all people. We bless
> thee for our creation, preservation, and all the blessings of this
> life; but above all, for thine inestimable love in the redemption
> of the world by our Lord Jesus Christ; for the means of grace,
> and for the hope of glory. And we beseech thee, give us that due
> sense of all thy mercies, that our hearts may be unfeignedly
> thankful, and that we may show forth thy praise, not only with
> our lips, but in our lives, by giving up ourselves to thy service,
> and by walking before thee in holiness and righteousness all our
> days, through Jesus Christ our Lord; in whose name we ascribe
> unto thee all honor and glory, world without end. *Amen.*

The General Thanksgiving has a venerable history. Using a prayer written in 1596 by Elizabeth I (1533–1603), the bishop of Norwich, Edward Reynolds, rewrote this as a prayer for the priest to say.

The phrase, "the redemption of the world by our Lord Jesus Christ," confronts us with a claim that may confound us, but one we cannot ignore, namely that Christ came into this world to live, die, and rise for God's kingdom, and to leave that kingdom to us as his risen "body." We are not called to explain that kingdom, but to live as if the kingdom has already come. How might we do that? We might begin by reading and contemplating the Beatitudes (Matthew 5:3-12), which are the guidelines for living in the kingdom of God.

Now the congregation says the concluding prayer.

> Almighty God, who hast given us grace at this time, with one
> accord to make our common supplications unto thee, and hast
> promised by thy beloved Son that, where two or three are
> gathered together in his name, thou wilt grant their requests;

fulfill now, O Lord, the desires and petitions of thy servants as
may be most expedient for them, granting us in this world
knowledge of thy truth, and in the world to come life
everlasting. *Amen.*

The wording is attributed to St. John Chrysostom ("the golden-tongued")
who was from about 344 to 407 CE the bishop of Constantinople, then the
capital of eastern Christendom. In writing this collect he drew from
Matthew 18:18-20, John 14:14, and I John 5:14-15. Later, he ran afoul of
the empress Eudoxia who sent him into an exile of incessant walking.
Already an old man, he died exhausted by this trial. His last reported
words were "Glory be to God for all things."

Now the minister says the benediction:

The grace of our Lord Jesus Christ, and the love of God,
and the fellowship of the holy Spirit, be with us all evermore.
Amen. (II Corinthians 13:14)

St. Paul often used this benediction to close his letters to young Christian
churches, and we use it to close many services of the church.

Some readers may be surprised to see a Trinitarian benediction
in the King's Chapel prayer book. We should remember that James
Freeman was a biblical as well as a rational Unitarian. Like such
predecessors in Europe as Michael Servetus, Francis David, and Faustus
Socinus, Freeman believed that a rational reading of the Bible
provided to Christians a sufficient rule for faith and practice. Because
this benediction is found in the Bible, the laymen on the 1785 committee
voted to keep it, though Freeman may have had his misgivings.

Note that no creed is said during the course of this service.
The 1785 prayer book of King's Chapel dropped the recitation of the
Nicene Creed during Holy Communion. In the next edition (1811)
the church removed the Apostles' Creed during Morning Prayer. Yet, as
noted earlier, this creed appears on the panels behind the
communion table as do the Ten Commandments and the Lord's Prayer.
As the Welcome to New Members (on page 120 of the prayer book)

states, "… we cherish the freedom to follow this tradition as we understand it."

Morning Prayer is followed by an offering, announcements, a hymn, a sermon, a closing hymn, a benediction, and a postlude.

Beginning in 1970, the children of the church school and their parents met at 10:00 a.m. in the Little Chapel of the parish house for a short, simple worship service. This service, which contained both prayer book and improvised material, was well received. Since 2015 this tradition continues under the title of Morning Light. The printed order of service features both traditional and contemporary hymns, chants, and prayers and uses currently spoken English. It is attended by both parish families and adults in our Beacon Hill neighborhood.

Midday Prayer
(Pages 19 – 23 in the prayer book)

Regular midday services are no longer held at King's Chapel. We include a short history of them, however, since the service is included in the prayer book.

In 1868 the Rev. Henry Foote initiated a midday service on the seven Wednesdays in Lent. Those services grew in frequency and attendance, reaching a high point in 1927 when daily services were being held October through May with an average attendance of more than two hundred.

These services attracted shoppers, passersby, office workers, and tourists as well as parishioners. They opened with a prelude, prayer, and hymn, and closed with a hymn, benediction, and postlude, but the sermon was the main feature. Attendance declined over the next forty years. By 1967 these services, then held only in Advent and Lent, attracted a handful of people. This may have been due to short and uncertain lunch breaks as well as a declining interest in preaching.

From 1967 to 2014, King's Chapel held midday services, at first on Wednesdays during Advent and Lent only. Later they were held weekly throughout the entire year. These services followed the previous model, but with less time for the sermon and more time for music and prayer. They attracted an average attendance of thirty to forty people. One key to their modest success was a light lunch served in the vestry afterwards. This provided an occasion to welcome visitors, discuss the sermon, develop lay leadership, and interest some worshipers in joining the church.

The midday services were discontinued in 2014 in favor of a 6:00 p.m. service of Holy Communion, held weekly on Wednesdays, except in the summer.

The 1986 prayer book provides two orders for a midday service, one as described above and a second penitential service that was used in Lent, which begins with this prayer of confession.

> Almighty and eternal God, who searchest the hearts of thy people, we acknowledge and confess that we have sinned against thee in thought, word, and deed; that we have not loved thee with all our heart and soul, with all our mind and strength; and that we have not loved our neighbor as ourselves. Help us, we pray thee, to blot out our misdeeds and to amend what we are; and of thine eternal goodness direct what we shall be, so that we may henceforth walk in the way of thy commandments, and do those things which are worthy in thy sight, through Jesus Christ our Lord. *Amen.*

The minister may then say the following prayer, which is derived from the 1552 prayer book.

> Almighty God, our heavenly Father, who of thy great mercy hast promised forgiveness of sins to all those who, with hearty repentance and true faith, turn unto thee; have mercy upon us, pardon and deliver us from all our sins, confirm and strengthen us in all goodness, and bring us to everlasting life, through Jesus Christ our Lord. *Amen.*

The minister leads the people in reading a psalm and saying the doxology. A member of the congregation then reads the lesson, which is followed by a short sermon.

The minister and people then read a set of versicles, often called "the little litany." It begins with a prayer for the congregation:

> *Minister*   O Lord, show thy mercy upon us;
> *People*   And grant us thy salvation. [Psalm 85:7]

For the civil order:
> *Minister*   O Lord, save the state;
> *People*   And hear us when we call upon thee. [Psalm 20:9]

For the church:
> *Minister*   Clothe thy ministers with righteousness;
> *People*   And let thy people sing for joy. [Psalm 132:9]

For all humankind:
> *Minister*   O Lord, save thy people;
> *People*   And bless thine inheritance. [Psalm 28:9]

For the poor:
> *Minister*   Let not the needy, O Lord, be forgotten;
> *People*   Nor the hope of the poor be taken away. [Psalm 9:18]

For peace:
> *Minister*   Give peace in our time, O Lord,
> *People*   For thou alone, Lord, makest us to dwell in safety.
>   [Psalm 4:8]

For the congregation:
> *Minister*   O God, make clean our hearts within us;
> *People*   And take not thy holy Spirit from us. [Psalm 51:10a, 11]

These versicles are followed by two or three brief prayers and the Lord's Prayer. The service ends with a hymn and benediction

Evening Prayer
(Pages 25 – 36 in the prayer book)

Until the mid-1800s Sunday was a busy day for King's Chapel parishioners. They attended Morning Prayer at 10:00 a.m., took a lunch break, and then attended Evening Prayer beginning at 2:00 p.m. in the winter and 3:00 p.m. in the summer. After the Civil War attendance at Evening Prayer began to decline. Although in 1918 the vestry voted to discontinue this service, the 1986 committee decided to keep the text in the prayer book.

Evening Prayer follows the same format as Morning Prayer but with some prayers and chants of its own. For example, in place of the General Confession, the minister could say "Let us in silence humbly confess our sins to almighty God."

The first prayer that follows confession assures us that a misplaced or excessive sense of guilt does not keep us from God's forgiveness. This prayer, which first appeared in a fifth-century service book, reminds us that our ancestors may, like us, have suffered at times from a too-demanding conscience.

> Almighty and everlasting God, who art always more ready to hear than we to pray, and art wont to give more than we desire or deserve, pour upon us the abundance of thy mercy. Forgive us the sin whereof our conscience is afraid, and grant us those good things which we are too ignorant to desire or not worthy to ask. This we ask for thy infinite mercy's sake, through Jesus Christ our Lord. *Amen.*

The second prayer is based on Psalms 51:1-3, 10.

> Have mercy upon us, O God, according to thy lovingkindness; according to the multitude of thy tender mercies blot out our transgressions. Wash us thoroughly from our iniquities, and cleanse us from our sins. For we acknowledge our transgressions, and our sin is ever before us. Create in us a clean heart, O God, and renew a right spirit within us; through Jesus Christ our Lord. *Amen.*

We have so far been unable to discover the origin of the following prayer.

> Almighty God, our heavenly Father, who of thy great mercy
> hast promised forgiveness of sins to all those who, with hearty
> repentance and true faith, turn unto thee; have mercy upon us,
> pardon and deliver us from all our sins, confirm and strengthen
> us in all goodness, and bring us to everlasting life, through Jesus
> Christ our Lord. *Amen.*

The people, led by the minister, now say the Lord's Prayer, then responsively the versicles, then the psalm for the day, and finally the following doxology:

> Now unto the King eternal, immortal, invisible,
> the only wise God;
> Be honor and glory, through Jesus Christ, for ever
> and ever. *Amen*

The Old Testament lesson is followed by either the *Magnificat* (Luke 1:46-55) or the *Cantate Domino* (Psalm 98), the New Testament lesson by the *Deus Misereatur* (Psalm 67) or the *Nunc Dimittis* (Luke 2:29-32). The text of the latter is as follows:

> Lord, now lettest thou thy servant depart in peace,
> according to thy word;
> For mine eyes have seen thy salvation,
> which thou hast prepared before the face of all people;
> To be a light to lighten the nations,
> and to be the glory of thy people Israel.

This chant appears as a prayer in Luke 2:22-28 where we read that the aged Simeon stood near the entrance to the temple in Jerusalem waiting for the appearance of the Messiah. When he saw Joseph and Mary bringing the infant Jesus to be dedicated, Simeon took the child from them and said the words we sing at this point in the service. He then prophesied the crisis that this child will bring to Israel.

The story continues with an account of Anna, an eighty-four year old widow, who also lived at the temple, praying and fasting. She also thanked God for the infant Jesus and told visitors to the temple that he would bring them redemption. (Luke 2:36-38)

Since the fourth century, Simeon's words have been sung at evening services to celebrate the incarnation of God's word in Jesus Christ and the light coming to Israel and the world. Like the Jewish people, Christians, despite our despair and disappointment, also pray that someday this world will become what God intended at its creation.

The prayer book provides for a sermon and hymn at this point followed by the same versicles that we find in Morning Prayer and followed by prayers, the first being the Collect for Peace.

> O God, from whom all holy desires, all good counsels, and all
> just works do proceed; give unto thy servants that peace which
> the world cannot give; that our hearts may be set to obey thy
> commandments, and that, being defended by thee from the fear
> of our enemies, we may pass our time in rest and quietness,
> through Jesus Christ our Savior. *Amen.*

This prayer is based on Jesus' words to his disciples, "Peace I leave with you, my peace I give unto you, not as the world gives, give I unto you. Let not your hearts be troubled, neither let them be afraid." (John 14:27) Unlike other prayers, this collect asks God to protect us, not from our enemies, but from our fear of them.

The following prayer, the Collect for Aid against All Perils, first appeared in a fifth-century service book during the reign of Pope Gelasius (492-496 CE). The words of this prayer, possibly based on Psalm 139:11-12, are worth repeating before one slips into sleep.

> Lighten our darkness, we beseech thee, O Lord, and by thy
> great mercy defend us from all perils and dangers of this night,
> for the love of thy Son, our Savior, Jesus Christ. *Amen.*

Following this collect are six prayers. The text of and the commentary on five of these—the Prayer for All Nations, the Prayer for All Who are in Affliction, the Prayer for the Clergy and People, the General Thanksgiving and the Concluding Prayer—may be found in the section about Morning Prayer.

The following Prayer for the Nation in the Evening Service replaces Morning Prayer's Prayer for Those in Authority. It was published in the 1914 *Services for Congregational Worship* by the American Unitarian Association.

> O God, the protector of all who put their trust in thee; we pray for the good estate of this our beloved land, that it may please thee to preserve to us the blessings of an equal and impartial freedom. Unite in mutual understanding those of alien race and faith; revive in all hearts a spirit of devotion to the public good, that strife and tumult may be stilled, that truth and justice be exalted. Enable us and all thy people faithfully to discharge the duties thou hast laid upon us, that thy kingdom may come and thy will be done on earth, as it is in heaven. *Amen.*

The 1986 edition put the Prayer for All Who Are in Affliction in place of the Prayer for All Sorts and Conditions of Mankind in Morning Prayer. It is found in the prayer book of the Church of Ireland, but its origin is unknown to us.

> Almighty and everlasting God, the comfort of all who mourn, the strength of all who suffer, let the prayers of those who cry out of any tribulation come unto thee; and may they rejoice to find that thy mercy is present with them in their afflictions. Let all who are beset by fears, troubled by poverty, worn by illness, all who are wronged and oppressed, the lonely, the suffering, the weary and heavy-laden, be sustained by thy might, consoled by thy tenderness, and cherished by thy compassion. *Amen.*

One of three benedictions is read. The first is based on II Corinthians 13:14 with which St. Paul closed several of his letters. It became a blessing in the early church and continues so to this day. Even though it names the three persons of the Trinity, it was included in the 1785 prayer book since it was biblical.

> The grace of the Lord Jesus Christ, and the love of God, and
> the fellowship of the holy Spirit, be with us all evermore. *Amen.*

In Numbers 6:22-26 we read that God told Moses to tell his brother Aaron to use the following words to bless the people, and thus it is called the Aaronic benediction. Aaron was the first priest of the Hebrew tribes. His male descendants inherited the right to priesthood.

> And now unto God's gracious mercy and protection we commit
> you. The Lord bless you and keep you. The Lord make his face
> to shine upon you and be gracious unto you. The Lord lift up
> the light of his countenance upon you and give you peace, now
> and for ever. *Amen.*

The third benediction was written by our affiliate minister, the Rev. Charles Forman (1920 – 1998), who said these words as he walked down the center of the aisle looking at members of the congregation as he passed them. When he reached the last pew, he turned and said the final words, "It keeps us all." This blessing is inscribed on a plaque in the church vestibule.

> The Lord bless you and keep you; the Lord keep all those whom
> you love, whether here or in some other place. May God be
> your companion and you be his friend, as you walk together
> through all the days of your life; and at the journey's end, may
> you find the welcome of God's love. It keeps us all. *Amen.*

Evensong

(Pages 37 – 45 in the prayer book)

The service of Evensong, added in 1986, begins with the following versicles and responses:

Minister Jesus Christ is the light of the world,
People   The light no darkness can overcome.
Minister Stay with us, Lord, for it is evening,
People   And the day is almost over.
Minister Let thy light dispel the darkness,
People   And illumine thy church.
Minister Let us pray.

These versicles were found in a post-Vatican II service book, *Morning Praise and Evening Song*, published by the Notre Dame Press. The first set are based on Jesus' statement, "I am the light of the world." (John 8:12, 9:5) The second set recalls the request of the travelers to Emmaus who, upon reaching an inn at the end of the day, asked Jesus not to leave them. (Luke 24:29)

The minister then reads one or more of the following prayers, the first of which was written by Lancelot Andrewes, successively bishop at the Chichester, Ely, and Winchester cathedrals in the early 1600s. Andrewes translated the first five books of the Old Testament from Hebrew into English for the King James Version.

Blessed art thou, O Lord our God, creator of the changes of day and night, giving rest to the weary, renewing the strength of those who are spent, bestowing upon us occasions of song in the evening. As thou hast protected us in the day that is past, so be with us in the coming night; keep us from every sin, every evil, and every fear; for thou art our light and salvation, and the strength of our life. To thee be glory for endless ages. *Amen.*

The following prayer appeared in *Orders of Worship*, published by The Lindsey Press in London in 1932:

> O thou who hast ordained that when the restless day is over
> there should come the quiet night; grant now thy rest unto all
> thy servants. Comfort and support all who must spend the hours
> of night in wakefulness through pain or grief or care, and all
> who must watch while others sleep. And when the night is
> ended, and the light of day returns, may we who have joined
> now in thy praise rise up with cheerful strength and gladness, to
> serve thee in all good works. *Amen.*

The next prayer comes from *The Apostolic Tradition*, a record of the rites and liturgical practices of the Christian church in Rome in the third century. It was compiled by Hippolytus, a priest and theologian who lived from 171 to 236 CE. He wrote many books, including *The Refutation of All Heresies*, and was a bitter critic of four popes. He was charged, but never convicted, of heresy for refusing to acknowledge that the holy Spirit was a person.

> We thank thee, O God, through thy Son Jesus Christ our Lord,
> through whom thou hast enlightened us. Night is falling and the
> day's allotted span draws to a close. The daylight which thou
> hast created has fully satisfied us, and yet of thy free gift now the
> evening lights do not fail. We praise and glorify thee through thy
> Son Jesus Christ our Lord, through whom be glory and honor,
> world without end. *Amen.*

At this point the congregation sings the first five verses as well as the eighth from Psalm 141 using the second verse as an antiphon, followed by a collect based on the antiphon.

> Let our evening prayers rise like incense before thee, O Lord,
> and let thy lovingkindness descend upon us, that with purified
> minds we may sing thy praise and glorify thee for ever and ever.
> *Amen.*

It was the custom in cathedral and abbey services for the celebrant at the end of a psalm to improvise a short prayer based on a single verse of that psalm. The purpose of these short prayers was to impress at least one verse of the psalm in the minds of the people. In his splendid four-volume commentary on the psalms, the great liturgist John Mason Neale (1818 – 1866) published several such prayers after each of the 150 psalms.

This particular prayer comes from the rich Mozarabic liturgies of the Spanish Catholic Church. Sadly, these were suppressed by popes Vigilius and Gregory VII in favor of the bare-bones Roman rite. The Mozarabic liturgy still continues in one chapel in the cathedral of Toledo. A wise cardinal secured this concession before Rome officially abolished the national rites of Spanish church. The Toledo rite and that of St. Ambrose in the cathedral of Milan are the only two non-Roman rites that continue in the Catholic Church.

The service continues with the reading of the psalm for the day, perhaps a collect for that psalm, then the doxology, and the reading of the Old Testament lesson. The congregation then sings either the *Magnificat* (Luke 1:46-55), or the *Cantate Domino* (Psalm 98). There follows the reading of the New Testament lesson and either the *Nunc Dimittis* (Luke 2: 29-32) or the *Deus Misereatur.* (Psalm 67).

Commentary on the Collect for Peace, the Collect for Aid Against All Perils, the Collect for the Clergy and People, and the Prayer for All Who Are in Affliction may be found in the section on Evening Prayer. The service ends with the Lord's Prayer and a benediction.

This version of evensong has been read at New Year's Eve gatherings at the King's Chapel parish house for several years. In 2015 an expanded service of Choral Evensong was held in the candle-lit church with a full choir and a cantor who led the congregation in singing antiphons. The service combines the traditional English format and language with imaginative thematic variations. It is planned to continue this rich liturgy on an occasional basis. Through such services as these the church evolves liturgically.

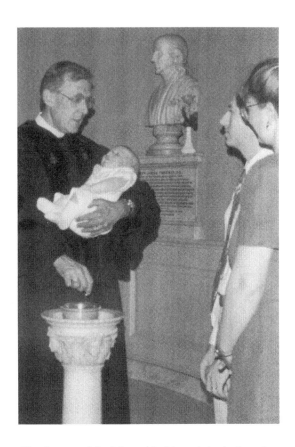

The Reverend Carl Scovel holds an infant whom he
has just baptized in the chancel of King's Chapel.

BAPTISMAL SERVICES

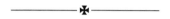

The word "baptism" comes from a Greek word, *baptizo*, meaning "to dip, soak, or bathe." A drunk was said to be baptized in wine, a spendthrift baptized in debt.

Long before the Christian era, pagan religions initiated candidates through rituals of bathing. The cult of Mithra required initiates to be bathed in the blood of a newly-slain bull. Judaism required adult candidates to take a ritual bath before conversion. The maverick preacher, John the Baptist, washed people who wanted to change their lives in the waters of the Jordan River near Jericho. (Luke 3:1-3, 7-14) All four Gospels report that he baptized Jesus.

The baptism of Jesus, not the pagan rites, became the rationale for Christian baptism. Inevitably, Christians would have held some kind of initiation ritual, for to become a Christian in an unsettled and hostile world was to change one's life, relationships, and future.

The first converts to Christianity were often baptized after hearing the preaching of such missionaries as Philip and Paul. (Acts 2:38, 41; 8:12; 16:15) At first they were baptized in the name of the Lord Jesus (Acts 8:16 and 19:5) or in the name of Jesus Christ. (Acts 2:38 and 10:48)

But so many early Christians showed such faith, courage, and devotion that they appeared to be moved by God's spirit within them. Before the holy Spirit was a doctrine it was a living reality among the first Christians. It is, therefore, not surprising that by 80 CE Matthew reported Jesus telling his disciples to "make disciples of all nations, baptizing them in the name of the Father, Son, and holy Spirit." (Matthew 28:19) This was the baptismal formula confirmed

by the bishops at the church's first general council held at Nicea in the
year 325 CE.

The church's first liturgical manual, written in the first century, called
the *Didache*, describes two ways of baptizing. It was done either by affusion
(water poured over the head of the baptizand) or by a three-fold
immersion. In both cases water was the essential symbol of regeneration.
The bishop, who at that time was the leading Christian priest in a given
city, was the only one authorized to baptize candidates.

Though most converts were adults, the book of Acts (16:15 and 33,
18:8) reports that St. Paul baptized whole households. Sometimes servants,
slaves, and children were baptized, not through their own conviction, but
in obedience to their parents or owners.

When Constantine made Christianity the de facto state religion in the
fourth century, the church suddenly became popular. Thousands of
families began to join the church. Suddenly baptism was not a risk to be
taken, but the thing to do. It became a custom, not a decision.

In time the church realized that candidates for baptism needed
instruction. During Lent, candidates fasted, prayed, and attended daily
services where they learned the basic teachings of the church by listening
to sermons. At the same time the already-baptized members of those
congregations received a refresher course in Christian faith.

We can read in translation many of these teaching sermons by
St. Augustine (bishop of Hippo from 395 to 430), St. John Chrysostom
(bishop of Constantinople from 398 to 404), and other church fathers.
After the sermon, the preacher blessed and dismissed the candidates.
The faithful remained to receive communion.

Candidates were usually baptized on Easter Eve or Pentecost in the
West and on Epiphany in the East. Just before the ceremony, candidates
gathered in a small chamber, called the baptistry, which adjoined the
main sanctuary. The priest asked them to renounce Satan and all his
works and to confess their faith in the words of the Apostles' Creed. The
priest then baptized them, usually by pouring water over their
heads three times. He then anointed them with oil and prayed that
God would send his holy Spirit into them. Candidates put on white
robes and entered the sanctuary to receive Holy Communion for the
first time.

During the Reformation such sects as the Mennonites, Hutterites, Swiss Brethren, and Baptists took a dangerous stand. They believed that baptism should be a conscious, mature decision. Therefore they baptized only adults, not infants or children who could not decide for themselves. Seeing this as heresy, Protestant and Catholic authorities alike hunted and murdered thousands of these courageous radical Christians. Yet these communities live and thrive today.

Becoming a Christian or becoming a particular kind of Christian can be dangerous. Candidates for baptism in countries and cultures in our time may risk their fortunes or their lives by taking this step. In this country Christians who take seriously their calling feel called to abandon or challenge the false gods of our own cultural corruptions. Whether one faces martyrdom, exclusion, or simply uneasiness, one does it in order to be transformed into one's lost and true self.

We cannot do this alone. We need a community, the family of Christ, the Christian church. Despite its failures, the church still holds out God's presence to us in scripture, worship, and in the lives of its martyrs, teachers, contemplatives, and saints.

Baptism is the door into a community where we belong to each other because all of us belong to God. John Donne, the seventeenth-century preacher at St. Paul's in London, put it this way: "The church is catholic, universal, so are all her actions. When she baptizes a child, that action concerns me, for that child is thereby connected to that head which is my head too, and ingrafted to that body whereof I am a member."

Although Catholic, Protestant, Orthodox, and Evangelical Christians are divided by doctrine, discipline, and admission to Holy Communion, virtually all of them accept each other's baptismal rites performed in the name of the Father, Son, and holy Spirit. Baptism, the rite of admission to the church, is the one rite on which they agree and practice true ecumenism.

Baptism of Infants
(Pages 47 – 51 in the prayer book)

Herb Davis, a United Church of Christ minister now retired, said, "To be baptized as an infant is to be carried into the church in the arms of another." To baptize a child is not only to give thanks for a precious gift, but to enroll this gift in a community where she or he will be named, known, held, loved, taught, and given a chance to grow into a community of faith.

Most Christian churches still baptize infants. This can be an act of faith or a formality. The faith of a child depends on the faith of his or her parents and congregation. God may plant the seed of faith, but the seed does not grow without the nurturing that parents, priest, and people provide. If they do not, baptism may become an immunization against faith rather than an introduction to it.

During its first three centuries the church required that adult candidates for baptism be sponsored by a member in good standing. This sponsor was known as the candidate's father or mother in God. By the fourth century, infants also needed a sponsor. The godparents, not the parents, brought the child to the church for baptism, held the child during the ceremony, and promised to teach the faith of the church to the child.

St. Augustine, bishop of Hippo in North Africa, wrote, "Infants are brought to receive spiritual grace, not so much by those into whose hands they are born, although they are brought by them also … as they are brought by the universal society of faith." Then as now, godparents represented both the congregation and the worldwide church.

When the child was older, the godparents, not the parents, taught the child the Ten Commandments, the Lord's Prayer, and the Apostles' Creed. These were deemed the essential texts of Christian faith. In many parish churches, as at King's Chapel, these texts were calligraphed on wood or canvas and placed over the communion table in the chancel. Those who come forward to receive Holy Communion may thus contemplate the three great texts of their faith.

When children were confirmed, they affirmed the vows their godparent took on their behalf at baptism. In the confirmation ceremony they might be asked to repeat the texts their godparents had taught them. Once confirmed, they could receive communion. In our day, godparents usually serve a nominal role, although a few take serious interest in their godchild's spiritual journey.

In the order for infant baptism, as in so many services, the Bible verses at the beginning set the tone and message for the service that follows. This service begins with God's commands to the Jewish people that they teach the commandments to their children. (Deuteronomy 6:4-7) The minister then reads the traditional baptism formula (Matthew 28:19) and the verses that tell how Jesus blessed the children. (Mark 10:13-16)

At King's Chapel there follows an exchange between the minister and the parents:

> Dearly beloved, you have brought this child here to be baptized;
> I ask therefore,
>   Will you instill into *his** young mind the knowledge,
> reverence, and love of God, as the heavenly Father of us all?

> *Answer*   I will.

> Will you teach *him* to live for others and not for *himself* alone; to
> do good to all; to abhor every form of falsehood, and to love
> what is just and honest, pure and true?

> *Answer*   I will.

> Will you exhort *him* to keep God's holy will and command-
> ments, and to walk in the same all the days of *his* life?

> *Answer*   I will.

> Will you instruct *him* in the Gospel of our Lord Jesus Christ, and
> teach him to follow Christ's precept and example, that *he* may
> learn to live the life that has no end?

> *Answer*   I will.

A charge to the parents reminds them of their responsibility. The first two charges were written by James Freeman. The 1918 edition dropped Freeman's third charge: "Will you exhort this child to renounce every thing that is evil, the vain pomp and glory of this world, with all covetous desires of the same, and the carnal desires of the flesh, so that he may not follow or be led by them?"

*The male generic is in italics, signifying that the minister should use the pronoun appropriate for the gender of the person.

The 1986 edition added a charge to the congregation. Before reading it, the minister reminds the congregation that as teachers, hosts and hostesses, friends, and parish leaders they should make their church a welcome place for children. If a child feels loved in a church, he or she will carry that love for the rest of his or her life.

> Will you, the members of this church and the whole Church of Christ, receive this child into your love and care, and will you uphold and encourage the parents and godparents in the fulfillment of their vows?
>
> *Answer*   We will.

At this point the minister says, "Name this child," and the parents speak the child's given name, reenacting the age-old association of someone's name with their essential being.

The minister baptizes the child in the name of the Father, Son, and holy Spirit, the universally-recognized words of initiation from Matthew 28:19. At the same time the minister marks the child's forehead with water in the sign of the cross, or pours water over the child's head three times.

In 1893 the Rev. Andrew Culp of Winchendon, Massachusetts, wrote a variant of the traditional form: "I baptize you in the name of the Father whose child you are, in the name of Jesus who loved little children, and in the name of the holy Spirit, which is promised to you."

The service concludes with one of two prayers asking for God's blessing on the child, and a benediction from Jude 1: 24-25.

> Now unto him who is able to keep you from falling, and to present you faultless before the presence of his glory, with exceeding joy, to the only wise God our Saviour, be glory and majesty, dominion and power, through Jesus Christ, for ever and ever. *Amen.*

In cases of emergency or necessity, where a priest or minister is unavailable, the church recognizes baptism by a layperson as valid.

Baptism of Those Who are of Riper Years
(Pages 52 – 55 in the prayer book)

"If someone has really found God through discovering Jesus Christ," a well-known Hindu wrote, "then that person must be baptized and show that he is a follower of Jesus Christ. Otherwise he is living a lie." That Hindu was Mohandas Gandhi (1869–1948), who understood from his own deep faith what it meant to obey God's call.

During the author's years at King's Chapel, he baptized thirty-two adults. Some were raised in Buddhism or Judaism. Some grew up in rational religious societies. Some came from no tradition. All were serious about becoming Christians.

The minister usually met with each candidate several times, first to hear his or her religious journey and subsequently to study and discuss the three basic texts of Christian faith, namely the Ten Commandments, the Lord's Prayer, and the Apostles' Creed. In the last interview minister and candidate reviewed the baptismal service itself and discussed what confession of faith the candidate would make. Some wrote their own, some picked the Apostles' Creed, and some chose the confession from the prayer book.

Here are the reflections of two adults who were baptized at King's Chapel:

> *"I believe my baptism to be an act of grace, a sign that I who did not seek God was found, and that the holy Spirit entered my heart to comfort and sustain me, and, in the words of Paul, to pray for me in those agonizing longings which never find words."*

> *"I went through the baptism mechanically and didn't feel too much beyond happiness that it was happening, so I was totally unprepared for what happened at the communion that followed. It was the most powerful feeling of power and unity present (almost a physical presence) as if it would be impossible to do anything wrong. But of course that is not describing it at all."*

In the order for adult baptism the minister reads the following words:

> Beloved of God, through the rite of baptism we enter the
> household of the whole Christian church and a new life in God,
> a life in which God forgives our sins, conquers death, and fills
> his people with the holy Spirit.

> Hear the words of our Lord Jesus Christ to his apostles:

The minister reads one or more verses from Matthew 28:19-20, John 3:5-6
and Acts 2:38-39, which provide the scriptural authorization for adult
baptism.

> John the prophet baptized Jesus in Jordan. Peter, Philip, Paul,
> and other apostles baptized Jews and Gentiles alike into Christ's
> death and resurrection. Early Christians baptized catechumens
> into the church. We repeat this act of initiation as a sign of
> forgiveness and rebirth, remembering the words of Paul to
> the Ephesians:

> There is one body and one Spirit, one hope of God's call to us;
> one Lord, one faith, one baptism, one God and Father of us all,
> who is over all and in all and through all. *Ephesians 4:4-6*

During the service the candidate and sponsor stand before the baptismal
font in the chancel. The sponsor represents the church, the people through
whom God draws seekers into the community of faith.

> *Minister* Who presents this candidate for baptism?
> *Sponsor* I do.
> *Minister* What is *his* name?
> *Minister* N.
> *Minister* N., is it your desire to be baptized?
> *Candidate* That is my desire.
> *Minister* Will you make your profession of faith?

The candidate makes a profession of faith either reading a personal confession, by saying the Apostles' Creed, or by answering the following questions:

Minister Do you believe in Jesus Christ as one who has
spoken words of eternal life?
Answer I do.
Minister Do you believe in that kingdom of God where the will
of God is done on earth, even as it is in heaven?
Answer I do.
Minister Do you now promise to obey the commandments
of God, as a disciple of Jesus Christ, and to make his
example the guide of your conduct and life?
Answer This I now promise and by the help of God will
endeavor to perform.

Then the minister shall say:

Will you, the members of this church and the whole Church of Christ, receive this person into your love and care, and will you uphold and encourage *him* in the fulfillment of these vows?

Answer We will.

The minister reads the following prayer:

Blessed art thou, O God, who hast blessed us with the gift of water. Over the primal waters thy spirit moved at creation's dawning. Through the Red Sea waters thou didst lead thy people, Israel, out of slavery to the land of promise. In the waters of Jordan, Jesus, thy Son, received John's baptism and was anointed by thy holy Spirit to lead us from death to resurrection, from sin to life eternal. Bless this people and especially thy servant, N., to be baptized through the gift of water that *he* may live in thee, and this we ask through Christ our Lord. *Amen.*

The minister then baptizes the candidate in the name of the Father, Son, and holy Spirit, and says one of these two prayers:

> Almighty God, the Father of our Lord Jesus Christ, regard in mercy the prayers of thy people; and bless thy servant, who hath now been acknowledged as a member of the Christian Church, by baptism. Incline *his* heart to receive with all readiness the doctrines and instructions of Christ, and to submit faithfully to the authority of his laws. Give *him* strength to triumph over the temptations of vice, and to be steadfast in the practice of that holiness which baptism is designed to represent; that, living as becometh a good and faithful member of the Christian Church here on earth, *he* may at length partake in heaven of that eternal kingdom which thou hast revealed to us by Jesus Christ our Lord. *Amen.*

> Bless, O Lord, thy servant N., and grant *him* the gift of the holy Spirit, the fire of faith, the breath of inspiration, the sense of unity with all earth's people. Grant that *he* may daily grow in grace and witness to that kingdom of righteousness which has no end, and this we ask through Jesus Christ our Lord. *Amen.*

King's Chapel's minister, the Rev. James Freeman, wrote the first prayer for the 1785 prayer book. The second was written for the 1986 revision. The service concludes with the benediction from the book of Jude 1:24-25.

Confirmation of Baptismal Vows
(Pages 56 – 60 in the prayer book)

Confirmation is the ceremony whereby Christians affirm the baptismal promises their parents or godparents made on their behalf at their baptism as an infant. The Oxford English Dictionary defines confirmation as "the rite whereby the grace of the holy Spirit is conveyed in a new or fuller way to those who have already received it ... at baptism."

The church knows that God's spirit can be neither contained and nor conveyed in a single ceremony. The gift of God's presence requires a life-long openness to God's will, made possible by worship, study, prayer, and witness. Confirmation is, therefore, a public profession of God's gift and one's serious desire to remain open to it.

In its early years the church had no confirmation service. When the bishop made his annual visit to each church in his diocese, he baptized all candidates who had been prepared. Immediately after baptizing each child or adult, the bishop laid his hands on the confirmand's head, prayed for the gift of God's holy Spirit, and then made the sign of the cross on his or her forehead with consecrated oil.

In 315 when Constantine established Christianity as a semi-official religion, candidates for baptism flooded the church in such numbers that the bishop no longer had time to baptize them all. Therefore, the local priest took over these responsibilities. At his annual parish visits the bishop confirmed these newly baptized Christians.

Children were baptized in infancy, but could not receive communion until they had been confirmed. This usually took place between the ages of seven and twelve, and that practice continues in Protestant and Catholic churches to this day. Only in the Eastern churches are infants as well as adults still baptized, anointed, and given communion in the same ceremony on the same day.

Some Protestant reformers rejected confirmation, calling it an "idle experience," since it was not commanded by Christ. They held that baptism itself admits one to the church. Protestants, however, often required their children to learn and recite a catechism. Currently many Protestant churches have some form of confirmation, usually administered to young adolescents.

King's Chapel's 1785 prayer book included a catechism written by Joseph Priestley. The 1877 edition included a confirmation service written by another English Unitarian, James Martineau. It was printed, said the introduction, "not as an obligatory service but as enriching the devotional treasures of this Liturgy, and to meet the desire, sometimes felt in the early freshness of religious experience, for an open form of Christian profession."

The 1986 prayer book added to the confirmation service more scriptural citations, the congregation's pledge to support the confirmand, an option for a personal confession in place of the printed questions and answers, and other prayers.

Confirmations have been rare at King's Chapel in the last fifty years. Four young women were confirmed in 1985, and three young men in the following year by the Hungarian bishop who was visiting Boston at that time. Nevertheless, at the Easter Vigil, the minister invites people to come to the communion rail and affirm their baptismal vows.

These versicles begin the Service of Confirmation:

Minister O Lord, open thou our lips;
People   And our mouth shall show forth thy praise.
Minister By one Spirit were we baptized into one body,
People   And all were made to drink of one Spirit.
Minister Now you are the body of Christ,
People   And individually members of it.
Minister If one member suffers,
People   All suffer together.
Minister If one member is honored,
People   All rejoice together. *I Corinthians 12:13, 27, 26*

Here the minister reads the words of Jesus in Acts 1:5–8, promising his disciples the gift of the holy Spirit, and then says:

Dearly beloved, inasmuch as you have signified your desire
to affirm the promises made on your behalf at baptism
[or reaffirm the promises that you made at baptism],
I ask you now in the presence of God and this congregation
to make public your profession of Christian faith.

The candidate makes a confession of faith and kneels. The minister and people say these versicles:

Minister The Lord be with you.
People   And with thy spirit.
Minister Our help is in the name of the Lord,
People   Who made heaven and earth.
Minister Blessed be the name of the Lord,
People   Henceforth, world without end.

Minister   Lord, hear our prayers,
People   And let our cry come unto thee.

The minister, laying a hand upon the head of each confirmand, says one of the following prayers. The first two appear in the Gelasian sacramentary and *The Apostolic Tradition*. Cranmer adapted them for the 1549 prayer book and Freeman adopted them for the 1785 edition at King's Chapel. The 1918 edition substantially revised them. The third prayer and the prayer for a child to be confirmed that follows it are found in *The Apostolic Tradition* of Hippolytus.

Almighty and ever-living God, the Father of our spirits, who delightest to do us good; strengthen, we beseech thee, *thy servants* N. with thy holy Spirit; and daily increase in *them* thy manifold gifts of grace, the spirit of wisdom and understanding, the spirit of counsel and might, the spirit of knowledge and true godliness. Grant this, O blessed God, through thy love to us in Jesus Christ. *Amen.*

or

Almighty and ever-living God, who makest us to will and to do those things that are good and acceptable unto thy divine majesty; we offer our humble supplications unto thee for *thy servants* N., who have made a public profession of *their* Christian faith, and expressed *their* earnest desire and prayer to be enabled to fulfill their duties as disciples of Jesus Christ. Let thy fatherly hand be over *them*; let thy holy Spirit ever be with *them*; guide and help, strengthen and sanctify *them*, we beseech thee; that, by the living bond of obedience and charity, *they* may be united to thee and thy beloved Son. *Amen.*

or

Strengthen, O God, *thy servant N.*, that *he* may continue thine forever and daily grow in the life of thy holy Spirit, until thou

shalt receive *him* at last in thine eternal home, through Jesus
Christ our Lord. *Amen.*

At the confirmation of children, the minister shall say the following prayer,
written by Thomas Cranmer for the 1552 prayer book. It is still read to this
day in the Anglican tradition.

Defend, O Lord, *thy child N.* with thy heavenly grace, that *he* may
continue thine forever, and may daily increase in thy holy Spirit
more and more, until *he* comes into thine everlasting kingdom.
Amen.

The minister reads one of three prayers and then leads the congregation
in the Lord's Prayer. Depending on the occasion, a brief homily or Holy
Communion and a hymn might follow. The service closes with the
following benediction from *II Corinthians 13:14*:

The grace of our Lord Jesus Christ, and the love of God, and
the fellowship of the holy Spirit, be with us evermore. *Amen.*

This print of Bishop William White administering the sacrament was designed by W. C. Armstrong and engraved expressly for *Godey's Lady's Book* by J. D. Gross.

Born in Philadelphia, Bishop White was the first Presiding Bishop (1785 and 1795-1836) of the newly formed Protestant Episcopal Church in the United States. He also served as the second United States Senate Chaplain.

HOLY COMMUNION OR THE LORD'S SUPPER

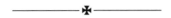

Holy Communion is a simple ceremony. The people stand, kneel, pray, sing, listen, and then in silence and reverence receive a morsel of bread and sip of wine. Why then have most Christians found it to be the essential act of worship for almost two millennia?

Its importance lies in what it signifies. The service itself is a suggestion of another meal, a meal that began in a rented second-floor room where a man about to be executed ate what might have been his last meal with his closest friends.

He was, in fact, killed and buried the next day. But oddly, and this too is fact, three days after he was buried, several followers, against their own expectations, became convinced that he had emerged from his death as a new kind of being in their midst. These friends in Jerusalem testified that they had seen and heard him, that he had eaten with them, and that he had spoken to them. Two others on the road to a small town west of Jerusalem said the same, and likewise others on a lakeshore north of the city.

What might have been dismissed as the delusion of grief-stricken followers turned into hope and energy in their conviction that not only had their rabbi (teacher) emerged from death, but that he now lived in them and that his life was their life too. Not surprisingly, most listeners called this folly.

His followers celebrated their conviction by re-enacting his last meal with them, which soon became their weekly worship service. Strangely, over three centuries more and more people were drawn into the community of his new life. And so today they gather in a service called "The Thanksgiving," or in Greek, the Eucharist.

It is called the Mass by Catholics and high church Episcopalians, the Liturgy by Eastern churches, the Qurbana (the Offering) in the Mar Thoma churches, and the Lord's Supper by Protestants and Evangelicals. As noted, the first Christians called it the Eucharist. In this book we will call it Holy Communion.

The earliest written account of Holy Communion appears in a letter St. Paul wrote to the Christian church in Corinth in 50 CE, only fifteen years after the Last Supper. St. Paul wrote, "For I received from the Lord what I also delivered to you, that the Lord Jesus on the night when he was betrayed took bread, and when he had given thanks, he broke it, and said, 'This is my body which is broken for you. Do this in remembrance of me.' In the same way also the cup, after supper, saying, 'This cup is the new covenant in my blood. Do this, as often as you drink it, in remembrance of me.' " (I Corinthians 11:23-26)

With these words Jesus broke with his own tradition when he added to the traditional Passover prayers, "This is my body which is broken for you," and "This is my blood which is shed for you." With these words Jesus pointed, not back in history to the Exodus, but forward to his imminent death, a death that would create a new exodus and a new Passover for his disciples. This exodus would lead his followers out of subjugation, not to Rome, but to the destructive powers of this world. This Passover would be their passport into a new kingdom.

St. Paul's report of Jesus' words are found almost verbatim in the first three Gospels' accounts of the Last Supper, written twenty to thirty years later. They show us how carefully the early Christians preserved and repeated his words, the seeds of the first Eucharist.

But it was not just the words of Jesus that Christians remembered. They also remembered his actions and what he did while he was speaking. Both St. Paul and the three Gospels report four actions: 1. He takes the bread. 2. He blesses the bread. 3. He breaks the bread. 4. He gives it to his disciples.

The Gospels report these four actions in another setting, the hillside feeding of a hungry crowd of four or five thousand people. There are seven accounts of these feedings, in which Jesus performs the same actions that he later does at the Last Supper. He takes, blesses, breaks, and gives the bread and fish to the people. It seems that Christians saw these hillside meals as precursors of his life-giving death and the Eucharist.

Over the following centuries these simple services (see Acts 2:42, 46 and 20:7a) evolved into the great masses of the medieval church, rich with processionals, choirs, and ornately vested clergy. The lay people, reduced to the status of spectators, shrank from receiving the host (the bread) even when it was offered, and never received the cup. Most of them took communion only once a year on Easter.

So strong was the precedent of this centuries-old abstention, that after the English church repudiated the power of Rome, the new Anglican bishops had to order the faithful to receive communion. In the 1552 and 1662 prayer books they printed the following direction: "And note, that every Parishioner shall communicate at the least thre tymes in the yere of which Easter to be one ..." In spite of this, most people continued to take communion only on Easter.

***

Following English precedent, King's Chapel at first celebrated Holy Communion only three or four times a year. But in the 1800s the church moved to monthly communions on the first Sunday of the month. Unfortunately, *The Annals of King's Chapel*, replete with dates, correspondence, vestry minutes, and reports of church conflicts, tells us almost nothing about how the congregation worshiped. After the departure of its Loyalist priest in the evacuation of Boston in 1776 and until the ordination of James Freeman in 1787, there were probably no celebrations of Holy Communion at King's Chapel.

Readers interested in this period of King's Chapel's history will find a brief summary under James Freeman in the Key Figures section of this book. A more detailed account appears in the previously cited *Journey Toward Independence* by Charles Forman and Carl Scovel.

The importance of Holy Communion in this church was challenged only once. In 1847 some members of the vestry proposed that the pulpit and reading desk be moved into the center of the chancel. The pulpit would thus have concealed most of the chancel.

That fall, the minister, the Rev. William Francis Pitt Greenwood, dismissed this proposal in a sermon, saying: "The most honorable portion of the church is allotted to the Communion Table, as the symbol of

Christian faith and fellowship. On one side of these precincts ... stands the pulpit, conspicuous, decent, ornamental, furnishing a convenient position for the instructor and leader in worship, but not the engrossing, prominent, and overshadowing fixture of the house. This is as it should be. A change which should transfer the pulpit to the chancel would in my opinion go very far to spoil the church and is such a change as I never wish to see in my lifetime and hope will never be made after I am gone." It wasn't, it hasn't, and, God willing, it won't be.

Holy Communion continued without interruption at King's Chapel until 1927, when an influenza epidemic in this country was taking thousands of lives. Anxious parishioners asked the minister, the Rev. Harold Speight, to discontinue offering the chalice, thus reducing the danger of contagion. Speight agreed, as he told the author, much to the relief of the parish. By 1933, when the Rev. Palfrey Perkins arrived, the epidemic had subsided, and the congregation received in both kinds again.

For most of its history the ministers of King's Chapel read the communion service from the north side of the table. Shortly after the Rev. Joseph Barth arrived in 1955, impressed with a Vatican II directive, he moved the communion table away from the wall and stood behind it, as he read the service facing the congregation. So it has been done since then.

In addition to first Sundays in the month, King's Chapel celebrates Holy Communion on Maundy Thursday, Easter Eve, Pentecost (or Whitsunday), All Saints and All Souls Sunday, Christmas Day, and New Year's Eve.

Since 2015, Holy Communion is also celebrated on Wednesday evenings in the candle-lit church. The service consists of hymns, chants with antiphons, prayers from several traditions, as well as the prayer book and the basic Eucharistic texts. A cantor leads the people in their responses, and they gather in the chancel for communion. This is an example of the kind of liturgical enrichment that enables a church to grow in its worship traditions.

For many years King's Chapel has welcomed to Holy Communion all who wish to receive. The precedent for this practice is found in the preaching and practice of the Rev. Solomon Stoddard, for fifty-five years (1675-1729) minister of the church in Northampton, Massachusetts. In contrast to his Puritan colleagues Stoddard welcomed non-members to communion because he believed that the communion service itself had the power to turn people to God. This is also our experience at King's Chapel.

The First Order for Holy Communion
(Pages 61 – 80 in the prayer book)

All orders of Holy Communion consist of two parts, the liturgy of the word, namely, the reading, celebration, and interpretation of scripture, and the liturgy of the table, namely, the prayers leading to communion and the reception of the elements. The two parts complement each other. Instruction prepares one for reception; reception instructs one in the reality of Christ.

In the First Order of Holy Communion, the liturgy of the word is Morning Prayer but without the prayers of confession and intercession since these will take place during the liturgy of the table.

The opening verses set the theme for the service. They are John 15:4-5, Revelation 3:20 and 22:17, John 6:35, I Corinthians 5:7-8 and 10:16. The minister then reads the Collect for Purity, a prayer that opens most Protestant and Catholic communion services:

> Almighty God, unto whom all hearts are open, all desires
> known, and from whom no secrets are hid, cleanse the thoughts
> of our hearts by the inspiration of thy holy Spirit, that we may
> perfectly love thee, and worthily magnify thy holy name,
> through Christ our Lord. *Amen.*

Morning Prayer continues with scriptural readings, chants, the collects for Grace, the Day, and Peace, and the General Thanksgiving. It ends with an offering, a sermon, and a post-sermon hymn.

The liturgy of the table then begins with the minister reading a prayer for the whole Church of Christ. After praying for those who confess the name of Christ, the minister often adds, "… and those who seek Thee by whatever name." The minister also remembers by name those in "trouble, sorrow, need, sickness, or any other adversity" as well as the recently departed, and then pauses for the congregation to remember their own friends or family.

Almighty and ever-living God, who by thy holy apostle hast taught us to make prayers and supplications, and to give thanks for all people; we humbly beseech thee most mercifully to receive these our prayers, and to inspire continually the universal Church with the spirit of truth, unity, and concord; and grant that all who confess the name of Christ may agree in the truth of thy holy word, and live in unity and godly love. We beseech thee also to bless all rulers and governors, and grant that all whom we place in authority over us may truly and impartially minister justice, to the punishment of wickedness and vice, and to the maintenance of true religion and virtue. Give grace, O heavenly Father, to all Ministers of the holy Gospel, that they may, both by their life and doctrine, set forth thy true and living word, and rightly and duly administer thy holy ordinances. And to all thy people give thy heavenly grace; especially to this congregation here present; that with meek heart and due reverence they may hear and receive thy holy word, truly serving thee in holiness and righteousness all the days of their life. And we most humbly beseech thee of thy goodness, O Lord, to comfort and succor all those who in this transitory life are in trouble, sorrow, need, sickness, or any other adversity [and especially thy servants . . . , and those whom we hold up to thee in silent prayer . . .]. And we also bless thy holy name for all thy servants departed this life in thy faith and fear, [and especially thy servants . . . ,] beseeching thee to give us grace so to follow their good examples, that with them we may be partakers of thy heavenly kingdom. Grant this, O Father, for thine infinite mercy's sake, in Jesus Christ our Lord. *Amen.*

Cranmer wrote this prayer for the 1549 (the first) prayer book of the Church of England. At King's Chapel James Freeman accepted this prayer but here and throughout the book replaced the word "sacrament" with the word "ordinance".

But how do we prepare ourselves to receive Christ's presence in Holy Communion? This is no casual question. In his previously quoted passage St. Paul goes on to say: "Whoever eats the bread or drinks the cup of the

Lord in an unworthy manner will be guilty of profaning the body and blood of the Lord. Let everyone therefore examine themselves, and so eat of the bread and drink of the cup. For whoever eats and drinks without discerning the body eats and drinks judgment upon himself." (I Corinthians 11:27-29)

Some churches require no formal preparation for communion. Orthodox and Roman Catholic churches require fasting, although in different degrees. Some churches ask parishioners to read pre-communion prayers. For many years the prayer book directed congregations to read the Ten Commandments before receiving communion. Most churches in that liturgical tradition, including King's Chapel, have the congregation say a prayer of confession and receive either a pronouncement of forgiveness or an assurance of pardon.

The act of confession at King's Chapel begins with the minister reading the following invitation:

> Ye who do truly and earnestly repent you of your sins, and are
> in love and charity with your neighbors, and intend to lead a
> new life, following the commandments of God and walking
> from henceforth in his holy ways, draw near with faith, and take
> this holy ordinance to your comfort, and make your humble
> confession to almighty God, saying with me:

The reader might notice the phrase "draw near with faith." In Anglican churches for two or three centuries most of the people left after Morning Prayer; only a few remained for communion. Since they were usually scattered through the church, the priest invited them to come near the chancel with the words "draw near with faith" in the invitation. Then came the prayer of confession, which the priest once read on behalf of the people. The 1662 prayer book directed the people, not the priest, to say:

> Almighty God, Father of our Lord Jesus Christ, we acknowl-
> edge and bewail our manifold sins, which we from time to time
> most grievously have committed by thought, word, and deed
> against thy divine law. We do earnestly repent, and are heartily
> sorry for these our misdoings; the remembrance of which is

grievous unto us. Have mercy upon us, have mercy upon us, most merciful Father. In the name of thy Son, our Lord Jesus Christ, we beseech thee to forgive us all that is past; and grant that we may ever hereafter serve and please thee in newness of life, to thy honor and glory, through Jesus Christ our Lord. *Amen.*

As noted elsewhere, succeeding editions of the King's Chapel prayer book dropped from the previous confession such words and phrases as "wickedness," "provoking most justly thy wrath and indignation," and "the burden of them [our sins] is intolerable."

One sentence in this prayer assumes a change in the hearts of the congregation, namely, "We do earnestly repent, and are heartily sorry for these our misdoings, the remembrance of which is grievous unto us." This raises a serious question. Can those who say this prayer at this point even remember their misdoings? In the Orthodox tradition the confessional prayer specifies sins as those "known and unknown, voluntary and involuntary, personal and collective." The prayer does not ask the congregation to express feelings of penitence at the time of recitation.

As in Morning Prayer, James Freeman, dubious of clerical authority, changed the priest's pronouncement of forgiveness to the minister's prayer for forgiveness.

Almighty God, our heavenly Father, who of thy great mercy hast promised forgiveness of sins to all those, who with hearty repentance and true faith, turn unto thee; have mercy upon us, pardon and deliver us from all our sins, confirm and strengthen us in all goodness, and bring us to everlasting life, through Jesus Christ our Lord. *Amen.*

As an assurance of our welcome to communion, the minister reads some or all of the following verses, called "the comfortable words." The word "comfort" (from the Latin *cum fortis,* "with strength") originally meant to strengthen.

Hear what comfortable words the Lord Jesus saith unto all who truly turn to him.

Come unto me, all ye that labor and are heavy laden, and I will give you rest. *St. Matthew 11:28*

God so loved the world, that he gave his only begotten Son, that whosoever believeth in him should not perish, but have everlasting life. *St. John 3:16*

Take my yoke upon you, and learn of me; for I am meek and lowly in heart, and ye shall find rest unto your souls. For my yoke is easy, and my burden is light. *St. Matthew 11:29-30*

Henceforth I call you not servants; for the servant knoweth not what his lord doeth: but I have called you friends; for all things that I have heard of my Father I have made known unto you. *St. John 15:15*

Peace I leave with you, my peace I give unto you: not as the world giveth, give I unto you. Let not your heart be troubled, neither let it be afraid. *St. John 14:27*

Or this:

Here also what St. Peter saith:

Ye are a chosen race, a royal priesthood, a holy nation, God's own people, that you may declare the wonderful deeds of him who called you out of darkness into his marvelous light. *I Peter 2:9*

Or this:

Hear also what St. Paul saith:

This is a true saying and worthy of all to be received, that Christ Jesus came into the world to save sinners. *I Timothy 1:15*

Then shall the Minister say with all the People answering:

Minister	Lift up your hearts.
People	We lift them up unto the Lord.
Minister	Let us give thanks unto our Lord God.
People	It is meet and right so to do.
Minister	It is very meet, right, and our bounden duty, that we should at all times, and in all places, give thanks unto thee, O Lord, holy Father, almighty, everlasting God;

This set of versicles is called the *sursum corda* from the Latin for "lift up your hearts." Clergy and congregations have said these words in preparation for communion since the year 200 when they were part of a Christian liturgy in Egypt. On holy days such as Easter and Pentecost, the minister reads special words of praise at this point. On ordinary Sundays the minister and/or the people stand and read or sing the following chant, the *Sanctus*, which is based on Isaiah 6:1-3:

Therefore, with angels and archangels, and with all the company of heaven, we laud and magnify thy glorious name, evermore praising thee, and saying,

Holy, holy, holy, Lord God of hosts,
heaven and earth are full of thy glory.
Glory be to thee, O Lord, most high. *Amen.*

Although at one time, only the minister said the following prayer, called the Prayer of Humble Access, the congregation now says it in unison. It is based on the conversation between the Samaritan woman and Jesus as found in Matthew 15:22-28.

We do not presume to come to this thy table, O merciful Lord, trusting in our own righteousness, but in thy manifold and great mercies. We are not worthy so much as to gather up the crumbs under thy table; but thou art the same Lord, whose property is always to have mercy; grant us, therefore, gracious Lord, so to

partake of this holy ordinance, that our minds may be
impressed with gratitude to thy dear Son Jesus Christ,
and that we may evermore dwell in him, and he in us. *Amen.*

The original prayer contained the phrase, "Grant us so to eat the flesh of
thy dear Son Jesus Christ and to drink his blood that our sinful bodies may
be made clean by his body and our souls washed by his most precious
blood." This text is based on John 6:53-56, where Jesus told his listeners,
"Unless you eat the flesh of the Son of Man and drink his blood, you have
no life in you. Those who eat my flesh and drink my blood have eternal
life." The text then reports, "Many of his disciples, when they heard this,
said 'This is a hard saying. Who can listen to it?' " (John 6:60) and the
account adds, "From that time many of his disciples drew back and walked
no more with him." (John 6:66)

Jesus, who has just called himself the bread of life, was saying through
the unforgettable metaphors of body and blood that what he gives people
is the very life within him, his own life, which is God's empowering
presence. Many of us, like the disciples who walked away, have lost the
capacity to read, hear, or think in metaphor and analogy. To literalists such
a text, and perhaps even the service itself, smacks of cannibalism. Perhaps
the King's Chapel congregation and editors in 1785 felt this way, when
they dropped the words from John's Gospel, and in their place put "…
grant us, therefore, Gracious Lord, so to partake of this holy ordinance,
that our minds may be impressed with gratitude to thy dear Son
Jesus Christ…"

The Minister, standing at the Table, shall read this account of
the Institution:

> The Lord Jesus the same night that he was betrayed took
> bread: and when he had given thanks, he broke it, and said,
> "Take, eat: this is my body, which is broken for you. This do
> in remembrance of me." After the same manner also he took
> the cup, when he had supped, saying, "This cup is the new
> testament in my blood. This do ye, as oft as ye drink it,
> in remembrance of me." *I Corinthians 11:23b-25*

These words of institution, as they are often called, are the earliest account of the Christian Eucharist, and therefore stand at the heart of every communion prayer. The phrase in the King James Version, "drink ye all of it," was once interpreted to mean that the bread and wine must be completely consumed. Later translations interpret the Greek original to mean, "All of you, drink this."

In place of the long prayer of consecration in the 1662 Anglican prayer book, King's Chapel's second Unitarian minister, the Rev. Francis William Pitt Greenwood, wrote the following prayer, which interprets communion as a memorial of Christ's crucifixion, through which we receive God's love:

Almighty God, our heavenly Father, by whose grace Christ Jesus
did choose to suffer death upon the cross; who did institute,
and in his holy Gospel command his disciples to continue a
memorial of his precious death; hear us, O merciful Father, we
most humbly beseech thee, and grant that we may receive this
bread and wine, according to the holy Institution, and in
remembrance of the death and passion of thy Son our
Saviour Jesus Christ. *Amen.*

In the 1662 prayer book, this prayer reads "our heavenly Father, who, of thy tender mercy didst give thy son Jesus Christ to suffer death upon the cross." The 1986 committee questioned the theology behind this phrase. For, if Christ shared our humanity, he shared our freedom and therefore the freedom to decide. He was God's Son, not God's puppet. He could have escaped his execution. For this reason the 1986 committee reworded Greenwood's prayer: " ... our Heavenly Father, by whose grace Christ Jesus did choose to suffer death upon the cross . . ." The ancient Orthodox liturgy catches this distinction with these words, " ... in the night when He was given up—or rather gave Himself up—for the life of the world."

This distinction has consequences for us. As disciples of Christ we are invited to choose God's will, yet God has created us free to refuse.

At this point in the service, while the choir sings the *Agnus Dei*, the ministers, who have been standing behind the communion table, pour the wine into the chalice, serve each other, and then come to the front of the table where they invite the congregation to come forward and receive with the words "The gifts of God for the people of God." These words are an interpretation of the Latin: sancta sanctis or "holy things for the holy."

In most celebrations priests and ministers have spoken certain words while distributing communion. The words in this service, "Take, and eat/drink this in remembrance of Christ" are derived from Luke 22:19 and I Corinthians 11:24-25.

"Remembrance" is an imperfect translation of the Greek *anamnesis* in the original text. *Anamnesis* means not so much the memory of a past event, as the re-enactment of that event so that it becomes real again whenever and wherever it is re-enacted. The whole service of Holy Communion is a re-enactment of Christ's life, death, and resurrection. The 1986 committee, however, unable to agree on a translation of *anamnesis*, kept the word "remembrance."

Ministers in the Unitarian churches in Hungary and Romania are silent when serving the elements to the people. The clergy simply look into the eyes of each communicant as they offer the bread or wine.

At this point, a psalm may be said or a hymn may be sung. Then we say the prayer Jesus taught his disciples. See the Components of Worship chapter for commentary on the Lord's Prayer. The minister then says this prayer:

> O Lord and heavenly Father, we thy humble servants earnestly
> desire thy fatherly goodness, mercifully to accept this our
> sacrifice of praise and thanksgiving; beseeching thee to grant
> that looking unto Christ and entering into the fellowship of
> his suffering, we may be changed into his likeness and with
> him pass from death into life. And here we offer and present
> unto thee, O Lord, ourselves, our souls and bodies, to be a
> reasonable, holy, and living sacrifice, humbly beseeching thee,
> that all we who are partakers of this holy communion may be
> filled with thy grace and heavenly benediction, according to
> thine abundant mercies in Christ Jesus our Lord; through whom
> all honor and glory be unto thee, O Father almighty, world
> without end. *Amen.*

This prayer is a substantially altered version of the post-communion prayer in the Anglican prayer book. The 1925 revisers added the lovely phrase, "looking unto Christ and entering into the fellowship of his suffering." This last phrase may have been inspired by Albert Schweitzer's conclusion to his then-recently published *The Quest for the Historical Jesus*: "… and to those who obey him, whether they be wise or simple, He will reveal himself in the toils, the conflicts, the sufferings which they shall pass through in His fellowship."

> In gratitude for God's presence in this service, we now offer "ourselves, our souls and bodies, to be a reasonable, holy, and living sacrifice" in words from Romans 12:2 and Philippians 3:10.

All shall stand and say or sing the Gloria:

> Glory be to God on high,
> and on earth peace, good will to men.
> We praise thee, we bless thee, we worship thee,
> we glorify thee, we give thanks to thee for thy great glory,
> O Lord God, heavenly King,
> God the Father Almighty.
> We bless thee for the life and Gospel of thy beloved Son;
> for all the gifts and graces of thy holy Spirit; and
> for the hope of life eternal.
> For thou only art wise, and holy, and good;
> thou only art the Lord;
> Thou only dost govern all things,
> both in heaven and earth.
> Therefore, blessing, and honor, and glory and
> power, be unto thee
> for ever and ever. *Amen.*

This ancient chant, an act of praise essential to every Eucharist, appears in a fifth-century liturgical manual, *The Apostolic Tradition*. See the Glossary for more information.

The minister then says one of these benedictions:

> The peace of God, which passeth all understanding, keep your
> hearts and minds in the knowledge and love of God and of his
> Son Jesus Christ our Lord; and the blessing of God almighty be
> among you, and remain with you always. *Amen.*

This benediction is based first on Philippians 4:7: "And the peace of God,
which surpasses all understanding, will guard your hearts and minds in
Christ Jesus."

> And now may the spirit that was in Jesus Christ be in us also,
> enabling us to know the truth, to do the will of God, and to
> abide in his peace.

The Rev. William Wallace Fenn, a Unitarian minister and the Dean of the
Harvard Divinity School from 1906 to 1922, wrote this benediction. It was
later inscribed on a plaque in the chapel of Divinity Hall in Cambridge.

The Second Order for Holy Communion
(Pages 81 – 93 in the prayer book)

There are two orders for Holy Communion in the prayer book. This raises
questions. Why is there a second order? And why did the revisers keep the
first? Both questions deserve an answer.

The 1986 committee had some concerns about the first order. It
seemed to them too penitential for what is, in fact, a service of thanksgiving. It also seemed more like a memorial service for a past Jesus rather than
a celebration of a present Jesus. The brief prayer of consecration in the
first order did not tell the biblical story of redemption, as do most communion prayers. In short, the first order seemed to lack the full sense of
thanksgiving that should be at the heart of a Eucharist.

At the same time the committee was not ready to abandon it
because it had served this church for almost three centuries and evoked
a piety we were not ready to abandon. The committee also knew
the second order would have to be tested by time, as had the first.

Guided by current Eucharistic reforms, the committee developed this second order.

It begins with the celebrant greeting the congregation with St. Paul's salutation to the young churches: "Grace to unto you and peace from God the Father and our Lord Jesus Christ."

The minister then reads the Collect for Purity (see the First Order of Holy Communion for commentary). The minister and people then say the following versicles and sing the *Gloria in Excelsis*, a hymn of praise that opens Holy Communion, not closes it as in the first order.

Minister O Lord, open thou our lips;
People And our mouth shall show forth Thy praise.
Minister Now to the one God, King eternal, immortal, invisible,
People Be honor and glory through Jesus Christ, for ever
and ever.
Minister Praise ye the Lord.
People The Lord's name be praised.

Glory be to God on high,
    and on earth peace, good will to men.
We praise thee, we bless thee, we worship thee,
    we glorify thee, we give thanks to thee for thy great glory,
O Lord God, heavenly King,
    God the Father almighty.
O Lord God of Sabaoth, God of our fathers,
    O Lord who gave us thy Son, Jesus Christ,
Who takest away the sins of the world,
    receive our prayer.
Thou who takest away the sins of the world,
    receive our prayer.
Thou who art the God of our salvation,
    have mercy upon us.
For thou only art holy,
    thou only art the Lord.
Glory be to thee, O God most high,
    through Christ and thy holy Spirit. *Amen.*

The minister and people read the psalm for the day, and then sing the doxology:

> Now unto the King eternal, immortal, invisible,
>   the only wise God;
> Be honor and glory, through Jesus Christ, for ever
>   and ever. *Amen.*

The people hear the Old Testament lesson and sing the *Te Deum* (see Morning Prayer), then hear the New Testament lesson and the sermon that follows. Thus, the sermon responds immediately to the lessons just read and may also look forward the communion itself.

After the sermon the people sing a hymn and read with the minister the following versicles, which sum up all the intentions of the longer prayer in the first order:

Minister	The Lord be with you.
People	And with thy spirit.
Minister	Let us pray. O Lord, show thy mercy upon us;
People	And grant us thy salvation.
Minister	O Lord, save the state;
People	And hear us when we call upon thee.
Minister	Clothe thy ministers with righteousness;
People	And let thy people sing for joy.
Minister	O Lord, save thy people;
People	And bless thine inheritance.
Minister	Let not the needy, O Lord, be forgotten;
People	Nor the hope of the poor be taken away.
Minister	Give peace in our time, O Lord;
People	For thou alone, Lord, makest us to dwell in safety.
Minister	Give rest to thy departed;
People	Let light perpetual shine upon them.
Minister	O God, make clean our hearts within us;
People	And take not thy holy Spirit from us.

The minister reads the collect for that Sunday and sometimes prayers for special occasions such as recent unhappy or joyful public events. On all Communion Sundays the following prayer, attributed to St. John Chrysostom, is read:

> Almighty God, who hast given us grace at this time, with one accord, to make our common supplications unto thee, and hast promised by thy beloved Son that, where two or three are gathered together in his name, thou wilt grant their requests; fulfill now, O Lord, the desires and petitions of thy servants as may be most expedient for them, granting us in this world knowledge of thy truth, and in the world to come life everlasting. *Amen.*

The minister and people then say the following confession followed by an assurance of forgiveness read by the minister. The proud and indifferent may feel they need no forgiveness, and the guilty may think they don't deserve it. Both need the freedom that comes from forgiveness, and the first step toward forgiveness is confession.

> Almighty God, Father of our Lord Jesus Christ, maker of all things, judge of all men, we acknowledge and bewail our manifold sins, which we from time to time most grievously have committed by thought, word, and deed against thy divine law. We do earnestly repent, and are heartily sorry for these our misdoings. The remembrance of them is grievous unto us. Have mercy upon us, have mercy upon us, most merciful Father. In the name of thy Son, our Lord Jesus Christ, we beseech thee to forgive us all that is past; and grant that we may hereafter serve and please thee in newness of life, to thy honor and glory, through Jesus Christ our Lord. *Amen.*

The minister then continues:

> Almighty God, our heavenly Father, has of his great mercy promised forgiveness of sins to all those who with hearty repen-

tance and true faith turn to him. I declare to you that he will have mercy on us, pardon and deliver us from all our sins, confirm and strengthen us in all goodness, and bring us to everlasting life.

People   Amen.

An alternate form of confession comes from the Liturgical Commission of the Second Vatican Council, in which the minister and people exchange the roles of penitent and confessor.

Minister   Beloved of God, I confess to you and to almighty God that I have sinned in thought, word, and deed; that I have not served God with all my heart and mind and soul; and that I have not loved my neighbor as myself. I therefore ask your prayers for me.

People   May God almighty have mercy upon you, forgive your sins, and bring you to everlasting life.

Minister   Amen.

People   I confess to you and to almighty God that I have sinned in thought, word, and deed; that I have not served God with all my heart and mind and soul; and that I have not loved my neighbor as myself. I therefore ask your prayers for me.

Minister   May God almighty have mercy upon you, forgive your sins, and bring you to everlasting life.

People   Amen.

Minister   The peace of God be with you.

People   And with thy spirit.

Minister   Let us praise God with our gifts.

At this point a collection is taken and an offering made for the work of the church. Since the church depends for its earthly existence upon the generosity of its people, as well as their labor and presence at worship, we should thank God at every service for those who support the church with their prayers, their labors, and their means. Here the congregation sings a pre-communion hymn.

Minister Lift up your hearts.

People We lift them up unto the Lord.

Minister Let us give thanks unto our Lord God.

People It is meet and right so to do.

Minister It is very meet, right, and our bounden duty that we should at all times, and in all places, give thanks unto thee, O Lord, holy Father, almighty, everlasting God;

Now the minister and people say the following words of praise, based on Isaiah's vision of God in the temple. (Isaiah 6:3) These words have been part of the Eucharist since at least the year 200. The final words beginning with "Blessed be he who cometh…" were the crowd's acclamation of Jesus as he entered Jerusalem before his final days. (Matthew 21:9) The word *Hosanna* means "Save us, we beseech thee."

Therefore, with angels and archangels, and with all the company of heaven, we laud and magnify thy glorious name, evermore praising thee and saying:

Holy, holy, holy, Lord God of hosts,
heaven and earth are full of thy glory.
Glory be to thee, O Lord, most high. *Amen.*

Minister Blessed is he who cometh in the name of the Lord.

People Hosanna in the highest.

The great prayer of thanksgiving that follows is so important that it warrants a short introduction. It consists of four paragraphs. In the first, we thank God for the sustaining gifts of creation, represented in bread and wine, through which we receive Jesus himself, our "daily bread."

The second paragraph reminds us of God's history with us; creating us, calling out to us through the prophets, and coming to us in the person of Jesus.

In the third paragraph the minister repeats the earliest words attributed to Jesus, creating the communion service itself.

In the fourth paragraph we thank God for the life given us through Jesus and ask His blessing on the bread, the wine, and us. Notice that we not only remember Jesus, but that in this service, we also reenact his life, death, and resurrection. The text of this prayer follows:

> All praise and thanks be unto thee, almighty God, for these fruits of the earth, this bread and wine, and for the life which thou hast given us through Jesus Christ.

> All praise and thanks be unto thee who made us in thine image and gave this earth into our keeping; who made a covenant with us and gave us thy commandments; who did not forsake us when we forsook thee, but sent us judges, kings, and prophets to call us back to righteousness; and who, when we persisted in rebellion, sent thy Son to be our Saviour. For in his days on earth he healed the sick, he fed the hungry, he rebuked the proud, he comforted the poor, and for the sake of our salvation he took the form of a servant.

> On the same night that he was betrayed he took bread: and when he had given thanks, he broke it, and said, "Take, eat: this is my body which is broken for you. This do in remembrance of me." After the same manner also he took the cup, when he had supped, saying, "This cup is the new covenant in my blood. This do ye, as oft as ye drink it, in remembrance of me." *(I Corinthians 11:23b-25)*

> All thanks be unto thee, O God, for Christ who gave himself to death upon the cross, who by thy power did conquer sin and death, became our peace, and renewed thy covenant with us. Reliving now his life, his death and resurrection, we offer thee this sacrifice of praise. Bless and sanctify with thy holy Spirit this people through these gifts of bread and wine, that Christ may live in us and we in him; and unto thee, O God, be all honor and glory, world without end. *Amen.*

The minister breaks the bread and pours the wine during the Eucharistic prayer or immediately thereafter, and then says one or more of the following words to the congregation:

> Come unto me, all ye that labor and are heavy laden, and I will give you rest. *St. Matthew 11:28*

> Behold, I stand at the door and knock; if any man hear my voice, and open the door, I will come in to him and will sup with him, and he with me. *Revelation 3:20*

> I am the bread of life; he who cometh to me shall never hunger, and he who believeth in me shall never thirst. *St. John 6:35*

> The Spirit and the bride say, Come. And let him that heareth say, Come. And let him that is athirst come. And whosoever will, let him take the water of life freely. *Revelation 22:17*

The ministers serve each other, and then, standing in front of the communion table, say: "The gifts of God for the people of God." The people come forward to stand or kneel at the rail, and the ministers distribute the elements with the words: "Take, and eat this in remembrance of Christ" and "Drink this in remembrance of Christ." When each row of people has been served, the minister says, "Go in peace." At the end of the distribution the minister and people say the Lord's Prayer, and then the minister reads one of the following prayers:

> O Lord and heavenly Father, mercifully accept our sacrifice of praise, and grant that looking unto Christ and entering into his fellowship, we may be changed into his likeness and with him pass from death to life. Here we offer and present to thee, O Lord, ourselves, our souls and bodies, to be a reasonable, holy, and living sacrifice, humbly beseeching thee that all we who are partakers of this holy communion may be filled with thy grace and heavenly benediction. For thine is the kingdom and the power and the glory for ever and ever. *Amen.*

The next two prayers come from the previously cited first-century manual for Christian worship called the *Didache*. The full name in English is *The Teaching of the Twelve Apostles*.

> We give thanks to thee, our Father, for the life and knowledge which thou hast made known to us through Jesus, thy servant: to thee be the glory for ever. As this broken bread was scattered abroad over the mountains, and being gathered together became one, so let thy Church be gathered together from the ends of the earth into thy kingdom. For thine is the glory and the power for ever. *Amen.*

> We give thanks to thee, our Father, for thy holy name which thou hast caused to dwell in our hearts, and for the knowledge and faith and immortality which thou hast made known to us through Jesus, thy servant: to thee be the glory for ever. Thou, almighty Father, hast created all things; both food and drink hast thou given unto us to enjoy, that we might give thanks to thee; and to us hast thou granted spiritual food and drink, and life eternal through thy servant. Before all things we give thanks to thee that thou art mighty: to thee be the glory for ever. Remember, Lord, thy Church, to deliver it from every evil, and to make it perfect in thy love; and gather it together from the four winds, the holy Church universal, into thy kingdom which thou hast prepared for it. For thine is the power and the glory for ever. *Amen.*

Just as Jesus and his disciples sang a hymn after celebrating the Passover, so we close Holy Communion with a hymn. The minister then dismisses the congregation as follows:

> Go forth into the world in peace. Be strong and of good courage. Hold fast that which is good. Love and serve the Lord with gladness and singleness of heart, rejoicing in the power of his Spirit.

The minister then says one of the following benedictions:

> The grace of our Lord Jesus Christ, and the love of God, and the fellowship of the holy Spirit, be with us all evermore. *Amen.* *(II Corinthians 13:14)*

> The peace of God, which passeth all understanding, keep your hearts and minds in the knowledge and love of God and of his Son Jesus Christ our Lord; and the blessing of God almighty be among you, and remain with you always. *Amen. (Philippians 4:7 and II Peter 1:2)*

> And now may the spirit that was in Jesus Christ be in us also, enabling us to know the truth, to do the will of God, and to abide in his peace. *Amen.*

The final benediction is the same as that which concludes the First Order. It was written by William Wallace Fenn.

The Third Order for Holy Communion
(Pages 95 – 100 in the prayer book)

This short form of communion was designed for use in homes or hospitals, and has the essentials necessary for a full celebration of that service. It is not replicated here because all of its parts have been described in the preceding commentary.

***

Recently a service of Holy Communion at 6:00 p.m. on Wednesday evenings has taken the place of the noon services on that day. It consists of praise, prayer, scripture, and sermon followed by communion open to all present.

This detail is from an etching by Paul-Adolphe Rajon of
"A Protestant wedding in Alsace" from the 1861 painting by Gustave Brion.

OCCASIONAL SERVICES

———————— ✠ ————————

Matrimony
(Pages 129 – 137 in the prayer book)

The first Christians had no church weddings. They were married before a magistrate in his office, not by a priest in a church. Their local congregation might pray for them on the Sunday following their marriage, but the ceremony itself was a civil affair.

By the fourth century, however, Christianity was becoming the state religion of the world once dominated by Rome. At the same time, Christian churches began to hold wedding services patterned on the old Roman traditions. At first these services were an option, but eventually Christians were required to get married in a church.

The marriage service in our prayer book is a descendant of the medieval ceremony established in England by the cathedral in Salisbury. The prayer book service, therefore, is the same text by which kings and commoners, paupers and professors, merchants and mendicants have been married for more than a thousand years.

Thomas Cranmer incorporated this ceremony into the 1549 *Book of Common Prayer*. It is a sober, thoughtful service, reflecting both the blessings and the responsibilities of marriage. The service assumes that it takes three to get married. Christ, who is God's presence, is the priest at a wedding and the couple's guide throughout a marriage.

The Puritans in England and America, like the early Christians, did not consider marriage a sacrament and thus were married before a magistrate. There were no ecclesiastical weddings in New England until

King's Chapel's first clergyman arrived in May of 1686. A few days later he married a couple who had been waiting for an Anglican priest and a church wedding.

After his arrival, James Freeman officiated at no services of Holy Communion, burials, or marriages until he was ordained in 1787. When he began conducting wedding services, he continued to use the Anglican service. However, it no longer included the bride's promise to obey her husband.

King's Chapel initiated the blessing of vows for those in same-sex relationships in 1994. The Massachusetts Supreme Judicial Court affirmed the legality of marriage for couples of the same sex in 2004. King's Chapel then began to perform weddings for such couples, with essentially the same service used for heterosexual couples. This congregation, like many others, understands that all couples who face the challenges of a committed relationship deserve the support of both church and state as well as the blessing of God.

A wedding, like all rituals of transition, marks the passage between a stage of life one is leaving, and that which one is entering. A couple who have met, fallen in love, and lived together for a year or more will probably look on marriage as a continuation of what they've already experienced— that is, an extension of their personal relationship. This relationship has provided them with mutual comfort, support, learning, and pleasure. During this period, either party can leave without legal constraint. At their wedding, however, they publicly agree to a state-sanctioned contract and a covenant before God, presumably for life.

Wedding services have changed. Once these services followed civil or religious tradition, but recently many have become more personalized, shaped according to the wishes of the intended. When such a couple decide to get married, they will likely, therefore, plan their wedding to reflect their own experience. They will choose the location, officiant, music, readings, and vows to express what seems to them at the time most real and important. They will also, understandably, want it to be happy and hopeful, vibrantly upbeat.

All this is to the good. Each couple is a unique entity, and the wedding service should reflect that. Furthermore, a wedding is a joyful occasion, deserving a grand celebration. Who would argue otherwise?

But something is missing at the unrelentingly upbeat wedding. Marriage is hard work, painful, frustrating, and confusing. A lifelong marriage demands a lifetime of maturation. The couple and the congregation need to be reminded that the two are making a contract that will try them sorely. The congregation needs to be told that these two people will require substantial help from family, friends, and others. The couple need to hear the admonition that to fulfill their life together they will time and again have to forgive or receive forgiveness, that to do this they will need the presence of the One before whom they made their vows.

One can learn this in a religious community, a kind of village where people teach each other. Those who live in such a village know they are marrying not just each other, but each other's families, cultures, values, and worldviews. They know they will need God's help as well as human help in making their marriage a state of mutual fulfillment and a home for others.

The context for their marriage will be not only their own experience but also the great body of human experience in marriage, as translated through a particular religious tradition. For us this tradition is found in the prayer book, whose service of matrimony we will examine.

Note that the language of this service is more formal than our usual discourse. This language is measured, cadenced, and serious, set apart from daily speech just as the ceremony itself is set apart from daily life. The author, having explained this service to hundreds of couples and read it at their weddings, has come to see that the language itself conveys both the solemnity of this couple's decision and its significance for the rest of their lives. This, if anything, makes their joy more significant.

***

The service of Matrimony is essentially a short worship service complete with prayers, hymns, scripture readings, and a brief homily.

First, the people arrive in a great and often chaotic bustle. Once they have settled down, the bride's father or her parents may escort her to the chancel. Sometimes the couple come down the aisle together. Sometimes both parents escort their respective offspring to the chancel.

The service begins with a preface reminding all present that this ceremony is taking place in the presence of God.

> Dearly beloved, we are gathered together in the sight of God and
> before the face of this congregation, to join together this man
> and this woman [or N. and N.] in holy matrimony, which is an
> honorable estate, instituted by God at the time of our innocency;
> which holy estate Christ adorned with his presence and first
> miracle which he wrought in Cana of Galilee. And, therefore,
> it is not by any to be entered into lightly or unadvisedly, but
> reverently, discreetly, soberly, and in the fear of God. Into this
> estate come these two persons now to be united.

The miracle just mentioned took place at a wedding banquet when Jesus changed the water in six large jars into wine. (John 2:1-10) We read that the master of ceremonies tasted the new wine and pronounced it a big improvement over that which had just been consumed. It seems that Christ intended everyone at that feast to be happy.

Immediately, there comes a pause before we continue moving toward the wedding vows. First, the minister says, "If anyone can show just cause why they should not be lawfully joined together, speak now or forever hold your peace." Suddenly, there is a silence, punctuated by nervous giggles. No one expects some killjoy to stand up and object, but everyone also realizes that they can't take this wedding for granted. No one objects, but again the minister raises another possible cause for concern. He says to the couple:

> I require and charge you both here in the presence of God that
> if either of you know any reason why you may not lawfully be
> joined in marriage you do now confess it.

Another pause, another silence, and again at least some people in the congregation realize that this couple is making an agreement whose consequences they cannot foresee. Let us assume the couple makes no response, so now the minister asks each of them the following questions, a rehearsal of the vows they will soon say:

N., wilt thou have this woman to thy wedded wife, to live
together after God's ordinance, in the estate of matrimony?
Wilt thou love her, comfort her, honor and keep her, in sickness
and in health, in sorrow and in joy; and, forsaking all others,
keep thee only unto her, so long as ye both shall live?

This is their first public promise. Any couple who have lived through
sorrow, joy, sickness, and health, know the hard work of loving,
comforting, honoring, keeping, and forsaking all others. We make
promises, we keep promises, we break promises. We forgive and ask
forgiveness, and the promise is renewed. All this takes place in God's
presence, whether we name God or not, whether we know God or not.

The minister has a question to ask of the congregation, for their
commitment is essential to the marriage:

Family and friends of N. and N., you who are about to witness
their vows, I charge you to stand by them, uphold them, and
make them the continuing gift of your love and prayers. Will
you accept this charge and so support them?

The congregation assents, and the minister asks, if it is pertinent, "Who
bringeth this woman to be married to this man?" Whoever did so, says,
"I do."

At this point in the service we hear a reading or two, at least one from
the Bible. The Old Testament offers some texts suitable for weddings. The
New Testament has no texts specific to weddings, but St. Paul's letters have
much advice on how to live in a community. People who marry become a
community. They become each other's first neighbor. Therefore, some of
St. Paul's instructions to new Christian churches may be good to hear
at a wedding.

After the readings the minister preaches a hopefully short
homily. Then the couple say their vows, the heart of the service, the public
profession of their commitment to each other.

I, N., take thee, N., to my wedded husband, to have and to hold,
from this day forward, for better for worse, for richer for poorer,

> in sickness and in health, to love and to cherish, till death us do
> part, according to God's holy ordinance; and thereto I plight
> thee my troth.

The ancient wedding vows end with "plight thee my troth," meaning, "I pledge you my trust." The couple promise "to love and to cherish." They do so, knowing that change is the only constant in life. Children come, dear ones die, jobs are lost, parents intervene, families move, sickness strikes. Through all these changes passion, affection, and cherishing come and go and come again. Trust is the basis for a long-term marriage.

The minister blesses the rings, and the couple say these words as they give the rings to each other:

> With this ring I thee wed, and to thee only do I promise to keep
> myself, so long as we both shall live, in the name of God. *Amen.*

The reader may notice four references to death in this service: "so long as we both shall live" in the pledge, "till death us do part" in the vows, "until their life's end" in the blessing of the rings, and "so long as we both shall live" in the exchange of rings.

These phrases remind us that one party will likely die before the other. That too is part of the contract, namely, that at some point one partner will live without the other.

Now the minister prays for the couple, expressing the affection, hope, and concern the congregation feels toward them. The minister prays first for the couple, then for children, and then for the family and friends, often adding the names of dear ones, absent or deceased. In 1986 we added the following prayer for the children of a previous marriage, written by our affiliate minister, the Rev. Charles Forman:

> Heavenly Father, we ask thy blessing upon the home to be
> established, and especially upon N., that [he, she, they] may feel
> secure in the affection that binds this family together. May they
> grow in love and loyalty, and in the years ahead have cause to
> thank thee for a home made safe by love and care, and this we
> ask through Jesus Christ our Lord. *Amen.*

The minister may or may not lead the congregation in reading the General Thanksgiving (see Morning Prayer), but almost always in the Lord's Prayer. These words, therefore, become the first words the couple say together after their vows. Acting now as an officiant of the state, the minister reads the following declaration of marriage:

> Forasmuch as N. and N. have consented together in wedlock
> and have witnessed the same before God and this company and
> have engaged and pledged themselves to each other, and have
> declared the same by the giving and receiving of a ring, by the
> exchange of vows, and by joining hands, I now pronounce that
> they are husband and wife. Those whom God hath joined
> together, let no one put asunder. And let all the people say
> "*Amen.*"

The congregation invariably responds with a resounding "Amen." Some form of this declaration comes from the medieval marriage ceremony, and must be at least a thousand years old. While the King's Chapel prayer book does not include the phrase, "by virtue of the authority vested in me by the Commonwealth of Massachusetts," the minister usually includes it. People are so used to hearing it, that they may question the legality of the wedding if it is not read.

The minister blesses the couple with the following words:

> The Lord God almighty bless, preserve, and keep you; The
> Lord mercifully with his favor look upon you, and fill you with
> spiritual benediction and grace; that you may so live together in
> this life, that in the world to come you may have life everlasting.
> *Amen.*

The minister then blesses the congregation with words from either Numbers 6:24-26 or II Corinthians 13:14. The couple embrace to loud applause and head for the reception and a new chapter in their lives.

Burial of the Dead
(Pages 139 – 146 in the prayer book)

At one time within present memory a casket, closed or open, was present at an end of life service, which consisted of scripture readings, prayers, and at least three hymns. The remembrance of the deceased was usually brief and in some traditions non-existent.

In the 1950s this began to change. More and more people began to see the presence of a casket, open or closed, as an unpleasant reminder of their mortality and a capitulation to the funeral industry. Cremations became more frequent, and caskets began to disappear. The new service included longer eulogies and fewer scripture readings, prayers, and hymns. The Burial of the Dead became A Celebration of Life.

Presently, most memorial services are focused on the virtues and accomplishments of the deceased. The congregation hears readings and music dear to or reminiscent of the deceased. Selected family and friends praise the deceased. Sometimes the officiant invites impromptu reminiscences from the congregation. The tributes are unfailingly positive. As one lawyer reputedly said, "The prosecution never gets a chance."

The effect of such unqualified encomia is to almost deify someone whose faults and failings were well known to their family, friends, and colleagues. For the deceased has not only blessed others, but has caused pain as well. Rarely at these services does one hear the thoughtful and, hopefully, forgiving acknowledgement that this person was less than perfect. Almost never does one hear a prayer asking God to forgive the sins of deceased against the living and the sins of the living against the deceased. Yet, if our God is merciful, and if we trust God's forgiveness, we should be able to remember the deceased as both saint and sinner, knowing that we too need forgiveness.

It is healing and right to remember and give thanks for our beloved. Never should we go back to the brief, sparse services of the past. The question is how far do we go in praising the dead, and what else do we do. There are two places where memorial services fall short.

First, they do not confront the congregation with the reality of death. There is no casket, little or no grieving, no solemn readings, hymns, or prayers, and no reflection of what it means for us, the living, to be mortal.

No one, it seems, wants a "morbid" service, yet morbidity is the very reason for our gathering.

This disinclination to deal with death is matched by a silence as to what happens after death. It seems that after appreciating the deceased there is little else to say. It seems that, although individuals at the service may believe in some kind of "afterlife," the congregation as a whole cannot agree on this, and therefore all should maintain an agnostic silence. This makes sense only when the congregation has lost a sense of the transcendent life behind our lives, our source, guide, and end of all our journeys on this fragile, lovely earth.

In contrast to this, a Christian burial is based on the transcendent truth of God's creation, providence, and purpose. This service, therefore, deals with three things: life, death, and eternity.

It deals with life, one life in particular, the person of the deceased, a unique child of God, one whom God created, guided, and loved in his or her time upon this earth. Therefore, we remember, appreciate, and reflect upon this person. We thank God for who they were and what they gave us, and we forgive their faults with us and ours with them.

It deals with death. The scripture readings remind us, in words we hear every Ash Wednesday, that we are dust, and to dust we shall return. The prayers and especially the sermon can deal with what it means to live a life filled with not only beauty and glory, but also with the little deaths we die with every loss and failure, and one that ends with our departure from this amazing gift of life.

The casket, urn, or even the photograph, processed to the altar at the beginning of the service and recessed to the narthex at its conclusion, is visible, tangible evidence that a real person has really died. I have seen members of the congregation, as they pass the urn or casket, touch it as a sign of affection and farewell.

It deals with eternity. Never does the text let us forget that all we do, say, think, and feel takes place in the context of God's transcendent love and purpose, however inscrutable that may be at any point in our lives. At the end of the service we commend the soul of the deceased to God.

***

The opening words in the order for Christian burial set the tone of the service with assurance and instruction from John 11:25-26, Isaiah 40:6-8, Psalm 103:13-14, I Timothy 6:7, and Job 1:21 and 19:25-27. These verses remind us that, like grass, we fade and perish. Naked we enter this world, and naked we leave. The One who gave us life also takes from us that precious gift, and yet receives us at the end.

Two prayers follow. One is from a medieval service, and the other is in St. Augustine's words, which are printed below:

> Infinite God, who cares so for each one of us as if for that one alone, and so for all, as if all were one; blessed are they who have loved thee, and their beloved in thee; for they alone lose no one dear to them, to whom all are dear in thee, who never can be lost. To thee we entrust all that we have received from thee, knowing that we lose nothing thou takest from us, who find our souls in thine encompassing light. *Amen.*

The congregation then sings a hymn, an affirmation of the church's faith and the people's hope. The people hear a reading from the Old Testament, say a psalm, and hear a second reading from the Gospels or Epistles. The choice of these readings is important. The instructive pessimism of Ecclesiastes, the confidence of Isaiah, the wisdom of Solomon, and the innumerable lessons of challenge and consolation from the New Testament speak to us when we are able to hear them.

The sermon that follows is the preacher's opportunity to set this death and all deaths, including those of the congregation, in the light of God's mercy, judgment, and providence, but above all, compassion. The Bible texts will guide the preacher in this regard, but the hearts, minds, and experience of the people present must be the preacher's main concern.

The sermon may be followed by memorial words from one or two well-chosen readers who know that each of us is a mystery like the God in whose image we are created. Therefore the speakers will say the significant and not attempt the comprehensive.

The prayer book provides at this point several prayers for the deceased. We have chosen five to reproduce here.

The following prayer was written by the Rev. William Huntington (1838–1909), an Episcopal rector, after he climbed Mount Sargent on Mt. Desert Island, Maine. The stunning view of the sea and surrounding mountains may have moved his muse, but he was clearly thinking of another mountain on that day.

O God, who on the mount didst reveal to thy chosen witnesses thine only begotten Son wonderfully transformed in raiment white and glistening, mercifully grant that thy servant, N., being delivered from the disquietude of this world, may be permitted to behold the King in his glory and all the beloved saints, world without end. *Amen.*

Another prayer, shortened from the original, was written by Francis Greenwood Peabody (1847–1936), son of King's Chapel's sixth minister and dean of the Harvard College chapel from 1886 to 1913.

Almighty God, speak to us all, as we gather here in common sorrow, thy solemn messages of life and death. Teach us to live as those who are prepared to die; and when thy summons comes, soon or late, teach us to die as those who are prepared to live; that living or dying we may be with thee, and that nothing henceforward, either in life or in death, shall be able to separate us from thy love, which is in Christ Jesus our Lord. *Amen.*

The following prayer comes from *The Priest's Prayer Book*, seventh edition, published in 1890. It is a collection of prayers for every conceivable liturgical and pastoral occasion compiled by Richard Littledale for priests in the Church of England.

Most merciful Father, who has been pleased to take unto thyself the soul of thy servant, N.; grant to us who are still in our pilgrimage and who walk as yet by faith that, having served thee with constancy on earth, we may be joined hereafter with thy blessed saints in glory everlasting; through Jesus Christ our Lord. *Amen.*

The following three prayers do not appear in the burial service, but were occasionally read by the minister when appropriate.

The first of these prayers for a child or an infant appeared in *The Priest's Prayer Book*, and in King's Chapel's 1918 prayer book.

> O God who hast made nothing in vain and who lovest all that thou hast made, comfort these parents in their sorrow and console them with the knowledge of thine unfailing love. Receive this child into thy merciful keeping, and this we ask through him who died and rose again to save us, even Jesus Christ our Lord.

A prayer for those in despair makes special mention of those who have taken their own lives:

> Remember, O Lord, in thy compassion those whose courage fails them in the moment of despair: when they begin to lose heart, renew their hope; when they are beaten to the ground, raise them up again; if they die by their own hand, forgive them, and forgive us all; and assure them both of thy love and of their own worth; and this we ask through our redeemer, Jesus Christ.

This prayer for the congregation came from the collection of Harry Stokes, a member of the 1986 prayer book committee:

> Almighty God, who hast made us to know that we are dust and to dust we shall return, make us also to know that we are temples of thy holy Spirit and recipients of thy grace, through Jesus Christ our Lord. *Amen.*

These prayers are followed by the Lord's Prayer and then a commendation:

> Go forth, faithful Christian:
> In the name of God who created you,
> In the name of Christ who died for you,

In the name of the holy Spirit which was given to you,
Go forth upon your journey from this world.
In communion with all the saints and the church triumphant
May you live in peace this day.
May your dwelling be in endless light,
And may you find your place in God's kingdom.

Minister May *he* rest in peace,
People   And rise in glory.

Then the minister shall read the following prayer either written by Henry Cardinal Newman or translated by him from the Latin original:

O Lord, support us all the day long of this troublous life, until the shadows lengthen and the evening comes and the busy world is hushed, and the fever of life is over, and our work is done. Then in thy mercy grant to us a safe lodging and a holy rest, and peace at the last. *Amen.*

An alternate prayer to Newman's is the *Nunc Dimittis* from Luke 2:29-32:

Lord, now lettest thou thy servant depart in peace, according to thy word; for mine eyes have seen thy salvation, which thou hast prepared before the face of all people; a light to lighten the nations, and the glory of thy people Israel.

The congregation stands and sings a final hymn, which should be strong and familiar. Then the minister reads one of three benedictions, the first from II Corinthians 13:14, the second from Numbers 6:24-26, or finally one based on Philippians 4:7:

The peace of God, which passeth all understanding, keep your hearts and minds in the knowledge and love of God and of his Son, Jesus Christ our Lord; and the blessing of God almighty be among you and remain with you always. *Amen.*

Words of Committal
(Page 147 – 151 in the prayer book)

In life the body and the person are one. At death they separate, and though it is now a spiritless body, we honor that body because it has been the earthly home of someone's soul.

Our humankind has different ways of honoring this separation. A Tibetan priest will chant from *The Book of the Dead*, directing the dying on how to find their way to the next world. Islam, Shintoism, and Judaism have rituals for washing and clothing the body for burial. Even in our "secular" age, when someone dies at home or even in the hospital, the family and friends may stay with the body, to sing, pray, reminisce, and receive visitors.

Whatever be these rites of honoring the body, we must then dispose of it. This happens through exposure to one of the four traditional elements—air, water, fire, or earth. Air: some Buddhists leave the body in a place where birds, wind, sun, and storm will consume it. Water: some burials take place at sea. Fire: cremation is now quite common. Earth: burial is still the usual option. In countries with limited space the body is buried only long enough for the flesh to disintegrate. The bones are then exhumed and placed in a charnel house where they too turn to dust.

Committals take place at sea, on a mountain, or in some other natural site, but still most often at a cemetery. The word cemetery comes from the Greek, *koimeterion*, which means "a dormitory." A cemetery, therefore, is a place where, just as we lived together, so we sleep together. For Christians, burial means both the reality of death (we do not slip immediately into heaven) and the promise of our awakening.

The committal service begins with the following scriptural sentences: Job 14:1-2, Hebrews 13:14, I Corinthians 13:9-10 and 12, and II Corinthians 4:16-18. These verses remind us that in the midst of life we are in the midst of death, and that in the midst of death we are in the presence of the One who created us and will receive us at the end.

A psalm is read, often the twenty-third, though others are appropriate. We might hear another reading at this point. If we are burying ashes, a member of the family will be asked to place the ashes, urn, or box in the grave. The minister then says:

Forasmuch as it hath pleased almighty God to take unto himself
the soul of his servant here departed, we therefore commit his
body to the ground; earth to earth, ashes to ashes, dust to dust;
in sure and certain hope of the resurrection to eternal life, when
they that sleep in the death of the body awake in the life of the
spirit; according to the mighty working whereby God is able to
subdue all things to himself.

We hear these words and remember that the earth is the body's origin and
destiny. Even if a body has been embalmed and sealed in a metal casket,
the earth will eventually have its way and reclaim its own, "for the dust
shall return to the earth as it was, and the spirit shall return to God who
gave it." (Ecclesiastes 12:7)

As the minister says the words, "earth to earth, ashes to ashes, dust
to dust," he or she throws a handful of dirt into the grave with each phrase.

When the body is to be cremated, the minister may say: "… we
thereby commit his body to the flames," followed by the rest of the
committal words.

The text of the cremation service first appeared in our 1918 prayer
book. Sadly, most cremations take place without a minister, friend, or
family member present. These words, therefore, are usually said at the
memorial service after the cremation has taken place. Some ministers
make a point of reading the committal service at every cremation in the
parish or arranging for someone else to do so.

The minister then reads Revelation 14:13. If a child is being buried,
Mark 10:14 is read. Several prayers may be read, including the following
adapted from the Eastern tradition:

Give rest, O Lord, to thy servants with thy saints, where sorrow
and pain are no more, neither sighing, but life everlasting.
Thou only, O God, art immortal, the creator and maker of all
mankind, and we are mortal, formed of earth, and to earth we
shall return. All we go down to the dust; yet even at the grave
we make our song, alleluia, alleluia, alleluia, to thee who art the
God of the living and the dead. Give rest, O Lord, and life
eternal, and this we ask through Jesus Christ our Lord. *Amen.*

Those present then say the Lord's Prayer, and the minister reads the commendation:

> Go forth, faithful Christian;
> In the name of God who created you,
> In the name of Christ who died for you,
> In the name of the holy Spirit which was given to you,
> Go forth upon your journey from this world.
> In communion with the saints and the church triumphant
> May you live in peace this day.
> May your dwelling be in endless light,
> And may you find your place in God's kingdom.

> *Minister*   May *he* rest in peace,
> *People*   And rise in glory.

This is our adaptation of the original words of commendation written by William Bright (1824–1901), a canon at Christ Church, Oxford. They come from his *Ancient Collects and Other Prayers*.

The service ends with one of three benedictions, II Corinthians 13:14, Numbers 6: 24-26, or the following adapted from Philippians 4:7.

> The peace of God, which passeth all understanding, keep your hearts and minds in the knowledge and love of God and of his Son, Jesus Christ our Lord; and the blessing of God almighty be among you, and remain with you always. *Amen.*

After the committal those present may throw a handful of dirt into the grave. They also may stay for a while at the graveside, sometimes for the lowering of the casket into the grave, but almost always for quiet conversation, visiting the nearby graves of family, or simply enjoying the beauty of the cemetery. For many mourners this is so dear a time that to hurry away would seem unkind as much to the living as to the dead.

The Visitation of the Sick
(Pages 123 – 128 in the prayer book)

Illness assaults not just the body but the heart, mind, and soul as well.
Illness brings fatigue, confusion, self-questioning, discouragement, and
even despair. For this reason the church has from its inception prayed for
the sick—for the mending of the body, the clearing of the mind, and the
healing of the soul.

King's Chapel's prayer books included services for offering communion to the sick, as well as visiting them, but in 1918 a new edition dropped
both services. The 1986 prayer book restored the Visitation of the Sick.
The service begins with a confession and an absolution and continues with
the 23rd and 130th psalms, followed by prayers. The service ends with the
Lord's Prayer and a benediction. This service may be said by a priest,
minister, pastoral visitor, or the patient.

The Welcome of New Members
(Pages 119 – 121 in the prayer book)

Prior to 1920, King's Chapel had no church members, as we understand
that term now. For more than two centuries the church was governed by
those who bought and owned pews in the church and paid an annual fee.
The Proprietors of Pews had the authority to call and ordain ministers and
elect wardens and members of the vestry, which served as the governing
board. Through these officials, they maintained the church buildings,
managed its finances, amended the prayer book, and, when necessary,
defended the church in court.

By 1907 most of the Proprietors had moved, died, or disappeared
without bequeathing their pew to another party. Given the rapid
decline of its legally constituted body, the remaining Proprietors created a
trusteeship by which three trustees would hold the church building and all
funds given for its maintenance "in perpetuity," a legal term not to be
confused with eternity.

In 1920, at the proposal of the Women's Alliance, 170 congregants
voted to create a parish organization called The Society of King's Chapel.
This body had the power to call and ordain ministers, elect officers, raise

money, manage the operating budget, direct parish life, and amend the prayer book. The 170 people who signed their name in the membership book thereby created The Society of King's Chapel. Since that meeting people have become members of the Society by signing that same book.

At the same meeting the Society adopted a covenant, based on a statement of faith written by the Rev. Charles Gordon Ames of Philadelphia and already in use by ninety Unitarian churches. The covenant reads, "In the love of truth and in the spirit of Jesus Christ, we unite for the worship of God and the service of man." Proposals for a word more inclusive than "man" suggest it is time to find an alternative.

When the Rev. Joseph Barth became the minister in 1955, he instituted a service of welcome for all who had joined The Society of King's Chapel in the previous year. The text of this service was incorporated into the 1986 prayer book.

The following portion of the service, read by the senior warden, the presiding lay officer of the church, succinctly describes King's Chapel's faith and practice:

> King's Chapel is unique: Unitarian Christian in theology, Anglican in worship, and Congregational in government. Through this church we belong to the Christian church around the world and to a tradition symbolized before you by the Ten Commandments, the Lord's Prayer, the cross of Jesus, and the Apostles' Creed. We cherish the freedom to follow this tradition, as we understand it, honoring both the freedom and authority of pulpit and pew. Here many generations have worshiped and now you, no less than they, become a part of its living tradition.

Thanksgiving Day

King's Chapel may be one of the few churches in our city that holds a worship service on the morning of Thanksgiving Day. We honor not just a national holiday but also the clear necessity of a good harvest if we are to live.

No one knew this better than the citizens of the Plymouth Colony after their first and devastating winter when half of their number died. The survivors, helped by their Native American neighbors, raised sufficient crops to justify an autumn feast, at which time they offered prayers of thanks for their survival. Such celebrations may well have continued in the colonies, but there was no proclamation of a national thanksgiving until 1786 when President George Washington declared November 26 the day for such celebrations.

Thanksgiving soon became a day for family gatherings, as Wendell Phillips testified in 1842: "Those who have wandered to other cities hurry back to worship where their fathers have knelt, and gather sons and grandsons to the littlest prattler under the roof … to cram as much turkey and plum pudding as possible."

Not until 1863 was another such day proclaimed, when Abraham Lincoln appointed the last Thursday in November as Thanksgiving Day. Only four years later, the Rev. Henry Foote, the newly arrived minister at King's Chapel, held the first Thanksgiving Day service at King's Chapel. In 1898 the vestry voted that services be held every Thanksgiving Day, and so they have since then despite holiday travel, football games, and family reunions.

From 1970 through 2016, Robert Hickling Bradford opened the service by reading one of two proclamations written by his father, Massachusetts Governor Robert Fiske Bradford, in 1947 and 1948. Governor Bradford, our senior warden for more than thirty years, was descended from William Bradford, the second governor of the Plymouth Colony.

Singing hymns and listening to an organ and choir are some
of the most satisfying parts of a worship service.

Saint Cecilia is the patron saint of music. This image, an 1890
"Fac Simile" of Hogarth's engraving, depicts the altarpiece of
St. Clements Danes, Strand, in London. It was ordered removed
in 1725 by the Lord Bishop of London "to prevent disputes and
the laying of wages" over its meaning. Some observers believed
they saw in the angel opposite St. Cecilia a depiction of the
Princess Sobieski, wife of the son of the exiled Stuart King James
II, the last Catholic king of England, and the mother of Bonnie
Prince Charlie, whose doomed rebellion in 1745
ended Catholic claims to the throne.

COMPONENTS OF WORSHIP

———————✠———————

Doctrine

Beneath every act of worship lies a set of assumptions as to who God is and how we come to God.

These assumptions may be stated explicitly or practiced implicitly, but they form a doctrine, which is the basis of the community's liturgy. This is true of Quakers, Catholics, Hindus, holy rollers, Muslims, Anglicans, and Sufis, among others. There is a saying, "Whoever grasps the little finger of liturgy will find they are holding the fist of theology."

Most Christian worship is based on a Trinitarian theology. To understand how this happened we must return to the beginnings of the church.

The New Testament is clear that Jesus felt a strong sense of communion with God. Jesus prayed to God as *Abba*, a term of intimate affection that meant "father" in his native Aramaic language. This became *pater*, the word for "father" in both Greek and Latin in all four Gospels. He prayed to this God in many states of mind—trust, distress, praise, and surrender. He spoke to his disciples, enemies, and listeners as one commissioned by this God. He offered God's presence through himself. The first Christians, most of whom were Jews like Jesus, knew God as Father from their own tradition.

Many whom Jesus preached to or healed, as well as his own disciples, heard not just wisdom from him, but felt God's presence in him. Some thought he was the Jewish Messiah, a heavenly military leader sent to save them from the Romans. Others, however, including St. Paul, saw him as God's son, sent to rescue them from sin and corruption. The crucifixion proved that Jesus was not the expected Messiah, but his resurrection convinced his followers that he was God's own son and therefore their savior. The birth stories in Matthew and Luke gave credence to his divine origin and mission.

The Gospels describe the disciples as not really knowing what Jesus was about while he was with them. They did not have his authority nor his close relationship with God. That changed on the day of the Jewish Pentecost after Jesus was no longer with them, when they experienced the holy Spirit in a dramatic way. The book of Acts (chapter 2:1-10) reports that more than one hundred disciples and other followers were moved by a heavenly power so great that it felt like "a noise like that of a mighty rushing wind," and they saw light like tongues of fire appear over each other's heads.

Then they felt God's power filling them as holy Spirit, and they began to speak and act, like Jesus, as people empowered by God. St. Paul, writing to the early Christian churches between 45 and 55 CE, makes one hundred thirty references to the spirit of God. It seems that God's spirit, given to the first Christians, became in itself a presence, living in them and yet apart from any one or all of them.

So the first Christians experienced God as the Father, the Son, and the holy Spirit. It was not a doctrine, but a living experience of how God became real to them. They did not believe these were three separate gods, but were all part of God's saving goodness. Within this Trinity there was an essential unity.

This Christian experience of God as Three in One became doctrine when ratified and elaborated by subsequent councils of the church, and later enforced by the state when Christianity became the official religion. The three became three persons sharing one substance.

Christians who questioned or modified this or other teachings were denounced in the anathemas of various church councils. The heretics were challenging not just the authority of the church but the doctrine of the Trinity itself. The church had been emphasizing the three persons of the Trinity to the exclusion of their unity, and claimed that the Bible itself taught Trinitarianism. The church had also focused on the divinity of Christ to the exclusion of his humanity. Finally, the church had so belittled human freedom and reason as to make the church institution itself the only means of salvation. The heretics aimed to redress what they considered theological imbalance.

Such heretics were subject to dismissal, imprisonment, exile, or execution. The first Christian to suffer the final penalty was Priscillian in 385 CE. Catholic rulers individually or collectively executed such heretics as the Cathari in the early 1200s. Protestants did the same to the Anabaptists in the 1500s. Against these persecutions rose protests from the likes of Desiderius Erasmus, a Catholic, and Sebastian Castellio, a Protestant.

One radical Protestant, Faustus Socinus, brought Unitarianism to Poland where a church based on his teachings, complete with parishes, a seminary, and publishing house, flourished until it was crushed by the Catholic monarch. In Transylvania, under the peaceable reign of King John Sigismund, a popular preacher, Francis David, founded a community of Unitarian churches that continues to this day in Romania and Hungary. In the late 1700s and early 1800s liberal preachers in England and America proclaimed Unitarian Christianity and created a family of such congregations. At the same time Universalist preachers carried the message of God's love to the farms and villages of New England and the Midwest. These preachers told their listeners that in time God would bring everyone into right relationship with Him. In 1961 the Unitarian and Universalist households in this country formed a single denomination, the Unitarian Universalist Association.

Unitarianism, the Christian belief in one God, can also be found in Jehovah's Witnesses, the Christian Science Church, the Church of Latter Day Saints, some Baptist churches and some members of mainline denominations.

What is the effect of doctrine on liturgy? We suggest that churches that take seriously the doctrine of the Trinity tend to celebrate highly developed liturgies, whose text is embodied in a prayer book. These churches are found in the Anglican, Orthodox, and Catholic households of faith. Many Christian churches hold nominal belief in the Trinity but to do not emphasize this doctrine. They tend to have simple orders for worship that include prayers, scripture readings, hymns, and a sermon, which may be the high point of the service.

King's Chapel may be an anomaly in that it has both a prayer book and a Unitarian Christian theology. It stands almost alone in a denomination that in the last century has moved from Unitarian Christianity to a broadly-based form of religion that draws on personal experience, nature, and several religious traditions, and has a strong concern for social justice.

Covenants, Confessions, and Creeds

Most but not all churches include the recitation of a statement of faith as part of their worship services. There are three kinds of statements of faith: covenants, confessions, and creeds. A covenant is a statement of faith made by a local church. A confession is a faith statement adopted by a federation of churches within a given nation. A creed, from the Latin *credo* meaning "I believe," is a statement adopted by a council of bishops with the intent that it be authoritative for the worldwide church and for all time.

The word "covenant" comes from the Latin, meaning "a coming together." A covenant is not just an agreement among people but a commitment made by members of a religious community to each other in God's presence. In congregational tradition such a covenant is made by the members of a local congregation, but in the Bible the whole people of Israel did this.

In the Old Testament it is God who initiates the covenant. God makes the first covenant with Noah (Genesis 9:1-17), the second with Abraham (Genesis 15:15-20), and the third with Moses (Exodus 1:1-6). After a history of covenants made and broken, God makes a new covenant with Israel as the prophet Jeremiah reports in 31:31-34. The first Christians saw themselves as people of this new covenant as reported in I Corinthians 11:23-26, II Corinthians 3:4-6, and Hebrews 8:6-13.

The first English settlers in New England saw themselves as people of the covenant. In 1629 those in Salem made the first such covenant in this country: "We covenant with the Lord, and one with another, and do bind ourselves in the presence of God, to walk together in all His ways as He is pleased to reveal Himself to us."

In King's Chapel's first century, its congregation said the Apostles' Creed at Morning Prayer and the Nicene Creed at Holy Communion. Gaining independence after 1781, it dropped that practice and continued without a faith statement until 1920. In January of that year the congregation formally organized as The Society of King's Chapel and adopted a revised version of the covenant written in 1881 by the Rev. Charles Gordon Ames, a Unitarian minister.

Ames' version of this covenant began with the phrase "In the freedom of the truth," alluding to Jesus saying, "If you remain in my word, you are really my disciples, and you will know the truth, and the truth will make you free." (John 8:31-32)

When the members of King's Chapel formally organized themselves into a parish in 1920, they changed the phrase "freedom of the truth" into "love of truth." The covenant that was approved now reads "In the love of truth and the spirit of Jesus Christ we unite for the worship of God and the service of man." It is time to find a more inclusive word than "man."

***

A confession is a provisional statement of faith, which the Protestant churches in a given country made to show where they stood in contrast to other Christian communions. A confession usually covers such belief matters as the nature of God and Christ, the human condition, the means of salvation, and the future of humankind.

The four significant confessions in Protestant history are the Augsburg Confession, made in 1530 by the German churches led by Luther and his colleague, Philip Melanchthon; the Helvetic Confession, adopted by the cantons of Switzerland in 1536; the Scots Confession, adopted in 1560 by the Scottish Reform churches under their leader John Knox; and the Westminster Confession, passed in 1648 by Parliament when England was ruled by the Puritans under Oliver Cromwell.

***

The first Christian congregations may have had their own statements of faith but in time they began to adopt the statements of larger and more influential churches. Such a statement was not originally called a creed, but a rule of faith or symbol. This precedent reminds us that the text does not itself contain the faith, but is a verbal witness to the faith of the church.

The most important question we can ask of a creed is why the church believed they were necessary. The first Christians had only a rudimentary sense of their identity. They knew they were children of the God of their Jewish heritage. They knew they were witnesses to Jesus Christ whom this God had sent to them. They understood that they were recipients of God's holy Spirit.

But the evolution of their identity did not stop there. The next stage of their self-discovery came from their encounter with a philosophical and religious movement called Gnosticism.

The Gnostics faced the same big question many religions ask: how could a good God create a world afflicted with suffering, evil, and death? The Gnostic answer was that God did not create this world. Gnostics taught that this world was created by a dismal, inferior, and ill-intentioned deity called the Demiurge, whom the Gnostics identified with the God of Judaism.

This Demiurge created a world of misery, shadows, and illusions, a world where life with God was impossible and therefore a world that one must escape in order to be with God. One could leave this world by spiritually ascending through many levels of angelic spirits until one reached the pure Supreme God. The Gnostics claimed that only their teachings, legends, and rituals could provide this means of ascent. That is why they were called Gnostics, which means "the ones who know."

Many Gnostics became Christians but they redefined Christianity to suit their already-held beliefs. They rejected the Jewish scriptures, especially Genesis, which taught that God created this world and saw that it was good. Gnostic Christians taught that Jesus was a purely spiritual being and could never have been human, for humanity, made of flesh, is corrupt. Therefore, they said, Jesus was never born, never suffered, never died, and so he never rose. Gnostics rejected the first three Gospels, which described Jesus' life as a human being. Furthermore, they accepted only parts of St. Paul's letters and parts of the Gospel of John.

Traditional Christians, on the other hand, claimed the Jewish scriptures as their own. Like Jews, they believed that creation was a witness to God's goodness as in Psalm 19:1, which says, "The heavens declare the glory of God and the firmament shows his handiwork."

Traditional Christians held that the Gospels were a true witness to Jesus, who was both human and divine and lived a real life in the flesh. In

John 1:14 we read "The Word became flesh and dwelt among us full of grace and truth." Christians believed that salvation was possible in this world, and that through their lives they must show God's love for this world, "For God so loved this world that He sent his only Son ..." (John 3:16)

The Gnostic movement attracted so many adherents within the church that traditional Christian bishops produced the Apostles' Creed, a definition of basic Christianity. This statement countered Gnosticism by stating, "I believe in God the Almighty, Maker of Heaven and Earth, and in his Only Son our Lord Jesus Christ, who was conceived of the holy Spirit, born of the Virgin Mary, suffered under Pilate, was crucified, died, and was buried, and on the third day rose from the dead."

If the Gnostics had won this battle, our worship service would be radically different. We would have no Old Testament readings, no psalms, no Gospels, no Christmas and no Easter, and no prayers for nations, rulers, the sick, or the suffering, for each person would be bent on his or her own salvation.

The Apostles' Creed became a confession that catechumens recited just before their baptism. The priest asked them three questions based upon the baptismal formula that Jesus directed in Matthew 28:19: "Do you believe in God? Do you believe in Jesus Christ? Do you believe in the holy Spirit?" The candidate for baptism answered each question in the words of the creed and thus owned the faith of the church as his or her own.

Although this creed does not include the word "trinity," it cemented the doctrine of the Trinity as the foundation of Christian belief in God. The creed took its present form in the ninth century and is now said at Morning Prayer in Episcopal and many other Christian churches.

The congregation of King's Chapel said the Apostles' Creed at Morning Prayer until it was abandoned by the second prayer book in 1811. It remains, however, inscribed on one of the four panels in the King's Chapel chancel.

The Nicene Creed was adopted by the bishops who met in Nicea in the year 325. It is the second authoritative statement of faith for the Christian church. Constantine called this council to settle a longstanding dispute among the bishops about the nature of Christ because he did not want such disputes weakening the unity of his newly established empire.

After much debate the council affirmed that Christ was of one essence with God the Father: "God from God, Light from Light, True God from True God, begotten, not made." The council condemned the dissident bishop Arius who held Christ to be a supra-angelic being and that "there was a time when he (Christ) did not exist." Unitarians used to claim Arius as their founder. The Nicene Creed is still said in Episcopal, Roman Catholic, and Eastern churches at celebrations of the Eucharist.

A third and much longer creed is attributed to Athanasius, bishop of Alexandria and Arius's opponent at Nicea. This Athanasian Creed begins with a warning that all who want to be saved must hold the faith described in the creed or face damnation. It spells out the essentials of "the catholic faith" in considerable detail. It is rarely in use now.

The creeds still define the basic parameters of Christian faith against the divisive individualism of the West, the escapism of excessive spirituality, and the nationalism of xenophobic cultures. That may be why most Christians in our day say a creed during their liturgy as a witness to the living God, to Jesus, God's Word made flesh, and to God's holy Spirit still living among them.

Hymns
(Pages 233 – 272 in the prayer book)

"Whoever sings prays twice," goes the old adage. That is the beginning of wisdom. Human experience and recent studies have shown that the act of singing is healing, energizing, and pleasing. When singing, especially with others, we intuitively commune with God and feel God's presence among us.

Jesus and the disciples sang a hymn before leaving the upper room. (Matthew 26:30) St. Paul enjoined us to sing. (I Corinthians 14:15; Colossians 3:16; Ephesians 5:18-19) The book of Revelation includes the texts of several hymns that were probably sung by the first Christians. (4:8,11; 5:9-10; 14:13; 15:3-4; 19:1-2)

St. John Chrysostom praised the power of sacred song with these words, "When God saw that many people ... had a hard time reading sacred texts, he wished to make it easy for them, and therefore added music to the sacred words, so that they, rejoiced by the charms of music, would sing to him with gladness." St. Augustine had never heard a sung liturgy until he went to Milan. In his Confessions he says that the bishop of the cathedral introduced singing "in order to prevent the people from succumbing to depression and exhaustion." He adds, "How I wept during those hymns and songs ... the music flowed into my ears and the truth was distilled in my heart. The feelings of devotion overflowed in me; the tears ran, and it was good for me."

Since Augustine's time the inherited Jewish chants of the early church have morphed into plainsong, polyphony, chorales, metrical psalms, anthems, spirituals, jazz, folksongs, and currently popular praise songs. These and other forms have enriched and enlivened the church's worship.

Singing does three things. It rejuvenates each singer. It unites a congregation. It fixes a text in the mind, mood, and memory of the worshipers.

Of course, only good singing has this effect. A strange or difficult tune, an odd or complex text, a pitch set too high or low, a painfully slow or maniacally brisk tempo, and, worst of all, a congregation unwilling to sing, can make a hymn the most distressing moment in the service.

Such musical disasters can be corrected only by leaders who want good singing because they themselves have experienced the power of praising God in song.

By Sunday afternoon the congregation will probably have forgotten the sermon, but if the service closed with a good hymn, the people will sing that hymn for the rest of the week. This may be why the Irish poet W. B. Yeats prayed:

God guard me from those thoughts
that think in the mind alone.
He that sings a lasting song
sings in the marrow bone.

King's Chapel's prayer book has been at times a hymnal. In 1828 the Rev. Francis Greenwood printed one hundred hymns from the Methodist and Moravian traditions. In explaining their presence, Greenwood wrote, "Their delightful fervor, though by some will be thought to be methodistical, will be thought by others, I trust, to be the true spirit of Christian devotion." These hymns stayed in the prayer book for ninety years until expunged in 1918.

In that year, King's Chapel published its own hymnal, which the congregation used until 1937 when the church adopted *Hymns of the Spirit*, published by the American Unitarian Association. The 1986 revisers included in the prayer book the text of thirty-eight additional hymns that the congregation had been singing in offprints.

The Lectionary
(Pages 479 – 550 in the prayer book)

A lectionary is a collection of daily, weekly, seasonal, or occasional schedules of selected scriptural passages to be read in the course of the church year. Our present lectionary is more than thirty years old. Its predecessor was more than a thousand years old.

The creation of a lectionary raises two questions: which texts will be read and when in the church year will they be read?

Judaism provided a precedent. In the time of Jesus the Jewish scriptures consisted of two sections. The first was the Torah, or the Law, also called the *Pentateuch*, meaning "the five scrolls." The Torah holds the heart of the Jewish people. It tells the story of creation, the early history of humankind, the emergence of the Jewish people, and the divine directives for them.

The second section is the Prophets, which includes three major, meaning longer, books, namely Isaiah, Jeremiah, and Ezekiel, and thirteen minor or shorter prophets, Daniel through Malachi. The Prophets also include the historical books of Joshua, Judges, I and II Samuel, and I and II Kings, since these books describe the work of such prophets as Elijah, Elisha, and Nathan.

A third section, the Writings, were not accepted as scripture until the year 100 CE. The Writings include the Psalms, the Wisdom literature (Proverbs, Ecclesiastes, Job) the Song of Songs, Ezra, Nehemiah, Esther, and Ruth.

Although the Torah, Prophets, and Writings constitute the Jewish scriptures, other books were accepted as scripture by some Jews and not by others. These books were Baruch, Bel and the Dragon, Ecclesiasticus, I-IV Maccabees, Judith, the Song of the Three Young Men, Susanna and the Elders, Tobit, and the Wisdom of Solomon. These books came to be called the Apocrypha. Although "apocryphal" now means spurious, its original meaning was "hidden."

The scholars in Jerusalem rejected these books, but the scholars in Babylon, the second great center of Jewish learning, accepted them as scripture.

The Jewish differences over these books continued in the Christian church. Presently, the Catholic Bible accepts all of the Old Testament Apocrypha except for Susanna and the Elders, Bel and the Dragon, and III and IV Maccabees. The Protestant Reformers rejected most, if not all, of them. However, many Protestant Bibles today include Ecclesiasticus and the Wisdom of Solomon.

At the time of Jesus there was no common schedule of readings. For this reason the reader in many synagogues chose whatever readings he preferred. Some congregations read through the entire Bible every year, beginning with Genesis and ending with Malachi. Some congregations read selectively. In time most congregations began to read certain books at festival seasons, such as Ruth at the spring harvest and Jonah on Yom Kippur, the Day of Atonement.

In our day most branches of Judaism follow a longstanding lectionary that specifies which portions of the Torah, Prophets, and Writings will be read during the religious year.

The first Christians, being mostly Jews, prayed in the synagogues and read the Torah and Prophets. Within twenty years after the resurrection, however, some churches were also reading St. Paul's letters, and, still later, portions from the emerging Gospels.

By the year 200 CE, Christian churches were reading the Gospels regularly, and by 300, the clergy had begun to read certain lessons on festival days and seasons, such as Isaiah's prophecy of the Messiah in Advent, the birth stories at Christmas, the Passion narratives in Holy Week, and the resurrection narratives on Easter.

In the 700s, the bishops in Rome, by then the authority in the Western church, decided on the following lectionary for the Old Testament and the New Testament Epistles:

Advent to Epiphany: Isaiah, Jeremiah, and Daniel
Epiphany to Septuagesima: Ezekiel, Job, and the Minor Prophets
Septuagesima through Palm Sunday: Genesis through Judges
Holy Week: Isaiah and Lamentations
Easter to Pentecost: the Epistles, Acts, and Revelation
Pentecost to Advent: I Samuel through Esther, Ruth,
    and the Wisdom of Solomon

In time the church's interest in scripture diminished due to the lack of educated priests and also to the medieval church's absorption in ceremony. The effect of this was to shorten scripture readings. For example, the sixteen chapters of St. Paul's letter to the Romans, which have 437 verses, were reduced to six readings of three verses each.

Thomas Cranmer in his preface to the 1549 prayer book described the state of affairs in England: "… since these many yeares passed this Godly and decent ordre of the ancient fathers, hath been so altered, broken, and neglected, by planting in uncertain stories, Legends, Respondes, Verses, vaine repetitions, Commemoracions, and Synodalles, that commonly when any boke of the Bible was begon: before three or four Chapters were read out, all the rest were unread."

It was the Reformers, that is, the Lutherans, Calvinists, Anglicans, Anabaptists, Zwinglians, and Moravians who restored the Bible to the center of Christian worship. Preaching became again the agent of conversion, instruction, inspiration, and pastoral guidance. The new medium of printing spread a preacher's message for miles beyond the sound of his voice and continued it for years after his death.

In England Cranmer created a new lectionary for the 1549 prayer book by combining one that Cardinal Quinones had devised for the Spanish church with another lectionary then in use at Salisbury Cathedral.

This 1549 lectionary provided an Epistle and Gospel reading for every Sunday and holy day of the church year. It also provided a schedule of daily readings from the Old and New Testaments, including most of the Apocrypha, but very little of the book of Revelation. Both schedules of readings were repeated every year. Only citations for Old Testament readings were given, but Epistle and Gospel readings were printed in their entirety.

For more than four centuries this lectionary was the standard for Church of England parishes in England and Episcopalian churches in the United States. Roman Catholic churches continued with the medieval lectionary. Protestant preachers chose their own texts.

The bishops at the Second Vatican Council (1962-1965) decided to reform their lectionary. Their charge read: "The treasures of the Bible are to be opened up more lavishly, so that the richer fare may be provided to the faithful at the table of God's word. In this way a more representative portion of the holy scriptures will be read to the people in the course of a prescribed number of years."

The new lectionary provided a reading from the Old Testament, the Epistles, and the Gospels for all celebrations of Holy Communion in each year of a three-year cycle. Many Gospel readings were paired with a related text from the Old Testament.

Matthew is now the Gospel read in Year A, Mark and parts of John in Year B, and Luke and parts of John in Year C. Whereas Catholic congregations once heard the same readings every year, they now hear more than 150 extended readings over three years. The new Catholic lectionary also provides a two-year schedule of daily Bible readings from both testaments for weekday church services and private reading.

Most Protestant churches never had a lectionary, but many of them began to adopt or adapt the Vatican II lectionary. The Presbyterians did so in 1970, the Methodists in 1976, the Episcopalians and Lutherans in 1977. In 1978 a committee of Catholic and Protestant scholars produced a revised Vatican II lectionary to be used in churches of both communions.

This was as astonishing as it was unprecedented. For the first time since the Reformation, Christians in thousands of Catholic and Protestant churches around the world were hearing the same lessons on the same Sunday. And in some communities these people were asking each other how their priest or pastor dealt with the text read on the previous Sunday.

The Catholic Church later revised the 1978 ecumenical lectionary for its own use. The Protestants, through the "Consultation on Common Texts," made their own changes in that lectionary. There is still a striking similarity between the Sunday readings in these two Christian traditions.

***

When James Freeman became the lay reader at King's Chapel in 1782, he inherited the lectionary of the Church of England. He read the lessons as prescribed, but like other New England divines he was as likely to preach on politics, natural disasters, historical events, and the doctrinal errors of his colleagues as on the lessons for that Sunday. For two centuries King's Chapel followed the Church of England lectionary, printing the full text of the Epistle and Gospel lessons in the prayer book. These lessons filled one-third of the pages in that book.

When the 1986 committee considered a lectionary for the new prayer book, they decided not to print the lessons. Instead they printed the schedule of readings that the committee of Catholic and Protestant scholars had produced in 1978. This included a three-year weekly schedule of readings for Morning and Evening Prayer and Holy Communion, a two-year daily schedule for devotional reading, plus lessons for such services as weddings, burials, ordinations, and certain festivals. In 2012 the vestry of King's Chapel voted to follow the recently revised lectionary that the "Consultation on Common Texts" had produced. This lectionary or its successor will likely appear in the next revision of our prayer book.

Litanies
(Pages 217 – 231 in the prayer book)

Litanies are extended prayers read or sung responsively between the priest and the people. They cover the same concerns as those raised in the shorter prayers, namely civil peace, public justice, the world, harvests, natural disasters, travelers, prisoners, the sick and suffering, the poor and oppressed, and, of course, the clergy and congregation.

The first litany in the King's Chapel prayer book is called the Great Litany. It may be read on the last Sunday of every month. This litany began as a much shorter prayer that was read in 1544 when Henry VIII led England into war against France and Scotland. Henry's liturgical deputy, Thomas Cranmer, expanded it by adding petitions from the Spanish, German, and other English service books.

The Great Litany begins with prayers for deliverance from inward and outward dangers:

From all evil and mischief; from sin; from the assaults of
temptation; and from everlasting destruction,
Good Lord, deliver us.

From all blindness of heart; from pride, vainglory, and
hypocrisy; from envy, hatred, and malice, and all
uncharitableness; from all inordinate and sinful affections
and from all the deceits of the world and the flesh,
Good Lord, deliver us.

From lightning and tempest; from plague, pestilence, and famine;
from battle, and murder, and from death unprepared for,
Good Lord, deliver us.

From all sedition, privy conspiracy, and rebellion; from hardness
of heart, and contempt of thy word and commandment,
Good Lord, deliver us.

The Great Litany continues with a series of intercessions asking for God's blessing on the church, its ministers, all civil leaders, and such concerns as the following:

That it may please thee to strengthen those who heal the sick,
lighten the sorrowful, and comfort the dying;
We beseech thee to hear us, good Lord.

That it may please thee to forgive our enemies, persecutors,
and slanderers, and to turn their hearts;
We beseech thee to hear us, good Lord.

That it may please thee to give and preserve to our use the kindly
fruits of the earth, so that in due time we may enjoy them;
We beseech thee to hear us, good Lord.

The 1785 King's Chapel prayer book shortened the Great Litany by discarding petitions for royalty and bishops and eliminating references to the incarnation, the Trinity, and Satan. This edition also directed that in this litany and throughout the prayer book all prayers formerly addressed to Christ now be addressed to God through Jesus Christ, "in strict obedience to his command." Freeman cited John 14:6 and 16:23, and numerous other verses from the New Testament as scriptural authority for this change.

In 1986 a petition was added for colleges and seminaries of learning, written by the Rev. Charles Forman, and a concluding collect written by King's Chapel's lay reader Harry Stokes. The governor was added to the list of leaders to be prayed for, and the phrase "or by air" to the prayer for travelers.

For centuries the King's Chapel minister led the reading of this litany with the people responding. But beginning in 1990, three parishioners in three different locations in the sanctuary took turns reading of most of the Great Litany, with the rest of the congregation responding as they had before.

***

The second litany is called a bidding prayer, since the minister bids the congregation to pray for a particular intention, and the people respond by reading a short prayer to that effect, as in the following examples:

Beloved of God, let us pray for the whole Church, the body of Christ:
Sanctify thy church, O Lord, that we may be one.

Let us pray for all ministers of God's word and especially for the clergy of this city:
Clothe thy ministers with righteousness, and let thy people sing for joy.

Let us pray for all the people of this world:
Lord, save thy people and bless us, for we are thine.

The third litany is an adaptation of prayers from the liturgies of St. Basil and St. John Chrysostom as found in the Episcopal 1979 *Book of Common Prayer*. Three examples follow:

> For those who travel by land, by sea, or by air; for strangers, refugees, and wanderers, let us pray to the Lord:
> *Lord, hear our prayer.*

> For the aged and infirm, for the widowed and orphaned, for the sick and all who are suffering, let us pray to the Lord:
> *Lord, hear our prayer.*

> For those who have died in hope, and for all the departed, let us pray to the Lord:
> *Lord, hear our prayer.*

The fourth litany is another bidding prayer also adapted from the 1979 Episcopal *Book of Common Prayer*. A short bidding by the minister is followed by a collect read by the congregation, such as:

> *Minister*   Let us pray for the Church:
> *Reader*   Almighty God, grant that all who confess thy name may be united in thy truth, live in thy love, and reveal thy glory to the world.
> *People*   Amen.

The fifth litany, a compilation by the 1986 revisers, is read in unison by the congregation. It begins with the Collect for Grace from Morning Prayer and concludes with the following prayer, attributed to St. Frances of Assisi (1181–1226):

> Lord, make us instruments of thy peace:
> Where there is hatred, may we sow love;
> Where there is injury, pardon;
> Where there is discord, union;
> Where there is doubt, faith;

Where there is despair, hope;
Where there is darkness, light;
Where there is sadness, joy.
Divine master, grant that we may not so much seek
To be consoled as to console;
To be understood as to understand;
To be loved as to love;
For it is in giving that we receive;
It is in pardoning that we are pardoned,
It is in dying that we are born to life eternal.

We also have the Litany of the Commandments. The Ten Commandments are also called the *Decalogue* (Greek for "the ten words"). Both Exodus 20:2-17 and Deuteronomy 5:6-21 report how Moses on Mount Sinai received from God these ten decrees, directing the Hebrew tribe how to live according to His will.

The first three commandments deal with a people's relationship to God. (1) They are to worship no gods but Yahweh. (2) They are neither to make or worship any image of God. (3) They are to hold God's name holy. In nomadic cultures a person's name was synonymous with their reality. Therefore, they are to live as if God were always present.

The next seven commandments direct human relationships. Two are positive. (4) God's people are to honor their parents. (5) They are also to keep a day of rest. The word "sabbath" means rest. Think of it! Even then people had to be commanded to rest.

Five commandments are negative, forbidding murder (6), adultery (7), theft (8), bearing false witness (9), and covetousness (10). Covetousness may be the last commandment because it is the root of the four preceding sins. Murder, adultery, theft, and bearing false witness all spring from the desire for someone else's life, spouse, goods, and reputation.

Clearly, Thomas Cranmer thought the Ten Commandments deserved a place in the prayer book, but where were they to go? Like other Protestant reformers, Cranmer believed that only those who had prepared themselves to receive communion should do so. St. Paul himself had warned his readers to examine themselves carefully to see if they were worthy to receive. "For anyone who eats and drinks without discerning the body, eats and drinks judgment upon himself," he wrote in I Corinthians 11:29-30. "That is why many of you are weak and ill, and some have died."

Some reformers required church members to make a personal confession to their minister before Holy Communion. Cranmer was less demanding. He thought it sufficient for the congregation to pray the Ten Commandments just before the communion service. Therefore, he directed the priest before communion to read the *Decalogue* to the congregation, the people responding to each commandment, "Lord, have mercy on us, and incline our hearts to keep this law."

James Freeman in 1785 moved the recitation of the commandments to the Sunday before Holy Communion and followed it with Jesus' summary of the law. (Mark 12:29-31) This gave the congregation a whole week to consider their worthiness to receive. The 1986 committee removed the reading of the commandments from Holy Communion and made it a penitential office to be read at the minister's discretion.

The Lord's Prayer

The only prayer taught by Jesus comes to us in two versions. In Luke's version (Luke 11:2-4) Jesus teaches a short form (without the concluding doxology) to be repeated word for word as a mantra. But in Matthew 6:8-14, Jesus instructs his followers to pray not in these words, but in this way, presumably using the prayer as a template. This is the one prayer that most Christians know well enough to say together.

Jesus prayed to God as *Abinu*, "Our Father," when he said the Eighteen Benedictions at morning and evening prayers in the Nazareth synagogue. These benedictions and several other phrases in the Lord's Prayer are found in Jewish tradition. Only the prayer for daily bread and for protection from temptation have no precedent.

The second-century manual of Christian prayer, the *Didache*, tells its readers to say the Matthew version of this prayer three times a day.

Orthodox congregations say the Lord's Prayer several times during a service; however, only the priest says the doxology at the end. At King's Chapel, as in most Protestant churches, the congregation says the entire prayer only once during a service.

The Lord's Prayer is a "we" prayer not an "I" prayer. Whether alone or in a congregation each of us prays as one of God's people, since Jesus taught us to say it in the first-person plural. We pray first for the coming of God's kingdom, then for ourselves, and finally for sustenance, forgiveness, and protection against the evils of this world. In Matthew's version we end with a doxology that proclaims that God is in charge.

Christians say this prayer not just at worship services, but also at baptisms, burials, weddings, deathbeds, and daily devotions. In the King's Chapel prayer book, the Lord's Prayer appears in every service, except for the two baptismal services and the welcoming of new members. Both usually take place after Morning Prayer when we have already said it.

The Offering

From its beginnings in 1686 the King's Chapel congregation took up a collection for the poor and such expenses as the priest's salary, the building of benches, and the purchase of communion wine. After the first church was built and pews installed, all church expenses were covered by the annual fees the Proprietors paid in order to retain ownership of their pews.

Collections, however, were still taken for the poor. At Sunday services the wardens passed among the pews collecting the people's gifts, while the clerk read verses from scripture encouraging generosity. These offerings assisted the poor of the church and the city. The church records report such payments as the following: "2 shillings for a poor man in necessitie, 2 pounds to Goody Tomlin for prison fees, 10 shillings for wood for an elderly couple, and 2 pounds 7 shillings to bury John Carter."

In 1828 the Rev. Greenwood proposed that the Easter Sunday collection be given to maintain a fund he and his successors could use to help the increasing number of poor in the city. So it was voted, and so it continues to this day with the addition of income from the Christmas collection.

In the late 1800s many Proprietors had moved, died, or disappeared, and the income from pew fees declined accordingly. For some time, legend has it, the church treasurer himself regularly paid the difference between the declining income from pew fees and the total of church expenses.

Perhaps collections had stopped because we read that in 1916 the vestry voted that a collection be taken at Sunday services. The vestry explained, "A collection is a customary part of nearly every church service, and many visitors to the Chapel have expressed their wish to contribute to its maintenance." In 1961 Rev. Joseph Barth proposed that the congregation sing the following refrain as the gifts were brought forward and placed on the Communion table:

> We give thee but thine own,
> What e'er the gift may be;
> All that we have is Thine alone,
> A trust, O Lord, from Thee.

So it was done, and so it is to this day.

Prayers and Propers
(Pages 153 – 216 in the prayer book)

A "proper" is a collect, preface, chant, or Bible verse designated to be read on a given Sunday or feast day of the church year. Each Sunday has at least one collect to be read on that particular day.

Each feast day has not only a proper collect, but also opening Bible verses specific to that day, a chant to be sung, and psalms to be read. In the event that the day falls on a Sunday when Holy Communion is held, there is a proper preface to be read just before the congregation says the *Sanctus*, "Holy, holy, holy."

Let us now turn to the prayers. Almost every edition of the King's Chapel prayer book has included prayers for those who might need a petition for particular times or events in their lives.

The 1986 committee gathered, read, and selected prayers that might suit this purpose. These included prayers before meals, prayers for morning, midday, work, and evening, and prayers for such occasions as births, anniversaries, journeys, sleep, illness, and the death of a loved one, as well as for other blessings and crises in a lifetime. This section also included prayers that could be read at parish events such as concerts and annual meetings and special concerns that might be raised at a Sunday service.

These prayers took up about twenty-five pages and were placed in the middle of the book, where they were and still are easy to miss. Many parishioners may not even know they are there. For this reason this guide has a special section, "Your Personal Prayer Book."

Psalms
(Pages 273 – 477 in the prayer book)

The psalms rise like a great chorus from the life of the Jewish people, from their exaltations and humiliations in the centuries before Jesus. When the Jewish scriptures were translated into Greek, the Hebrew word for sacred song, *mizmor*, became *psalmoi*, which became psalm in English.

Though many psalms are attributed to a specific author (seventy-three to King David alone), the writers of the other psalms are unknown, and David's authorship is seriously disputed. The psalmists' anonymity checks our curiosity. Far more important than those who wrote them are those who have read and sung them for more than two millennia.

After the Jewish exiles returned from Babylon and rebuilt the temple in Jerusalem, the psalms they had sung in Babylon (see Psalm 137) continued to be part of temple worship. When the guilds of priests processed around the altar of the temple, accompanied by an orchestra of harps, lyres, pipes, horns, trumpets, and cymbals, they chanted such psalms as 24, 132 and 150. Chapter 50:11-21 of Ecclesiasticus (not Ecclesiastes) describes these dramatic processions and sacrifices.

Many Jews, however, did not stay in Jerusalem but returned to the towns and villages of Judea. There they resumed the services of song, prayer, and scripture study that had sustained them in exile.

Every morning and evening, while the priests in Jerusalem were offering sacrifices in the temple, the faithful who lived in these towns and villages gathered for prayer in their local synagogues. And the songs they read or chanted there were the psalms.

Since many could not read, the psalms may have been sung antiphonally. The cantor would teach the people a single verse of a psalm, which they sang in response to the verses the cantor sang. This verse was called the *antiphon*.

Jesus learned the psalms in the Nazareth synagogue, and he knew them well, for he quoted them throughout his ministry. Two of his seven last utterances were from the psalms. (22:1 and 31:5)

The prayers of the Jews became the hymns of the first Christians. The New Testament has ninety-three quotations from more than sixty psalms. St. Paul tells the Christians in Colossus to sing "psalms, hymns, and spiritual songs." He and St. Peter quoted the psalms when preaching in synagogues. Psalm 118, the great Passover psalm of the Jews, became the psalm Christians sang on *Pascha* (Easter), the Christian Passover.

The monks living in the Syrian and Egyptian deserts chanted the psalms when they met for worship, often singing all 150 psalms in a single week as many abbeys do today. When Benedict of Nursia wrote the rule for the abbey he founded at Monte Cassino in the early 500s, he specified that his monks worship eight times a day. These short daily services, called offices, consisted of psalms, prayers, and a short scripture reading. Benedict specified that all 150 psalms be sung or read in the course of a month.

The psalms were important not just to monks but to local congregations as well and were used especially by the Protestant reformers. Martin Luther in Germany and Protestant leaders in Switzerland, France, and England wrote metrical versions of the psalms to be sung to local folk melodies. Thomas Cranmer in England followed the medieval pattern of reading or chanting psalms. In the 1549 prayer book Cranmer directed all congregations in England to read the entire Psalter in the course of a month.

James Freeman and his remnant King's Chapel congregation in 1785 inherited the 1662 prayer book from their Anglican forebears. Like their Anglican predecessors they divided the psalms into thirty-one sections, the maximum number of days in a month. On a given Sunday they read the two, three, or four psalms appointed for the day of the month on which that Sunday fell. Thus, in the course of year the congregation might read the entire Psalter several times.

Like other congregations, the people at King's Chapel have found many psalms and portions of other psalms difficult to read as part of their worship. The bitter invective against enemies and the pleas for God to destroy them contradict the letter and spirit of Christ's preaching. For this reason the psalms have had bumpy history during the nine revisions of the King's Chapel prayer book.

In his preface to the 1785 edition, Freeman wrote "A few passages in the Psalter, which are liable to be misconstrued or misapplied, are printed in italics, and are designed to be omitted...." Freeman's omissions included calls upon God to punish or destroy the ungodly, as in Psalm 144:6: "Cast forth thy lightning and tear them; shoot out thine arrows, and consume them," or 83:17: "Let them be put to shame and perish."

The 1828 prayer book did not italicize the offending portions, but deleted forty psalms entirely and portions of other psalms. Duplications in text, references to historical events, pleas to a wrathful God, imprecations against enemies, and exultations over their destruction were all deemed just cause for excision. Subsequent editions omitted or readmitted various psalms.

The effect of all this was that in 1981 when a new committee began work on the next edition, forty-five psalms had been cut in their entirety, thirty five had been radically edited, and thirty-three others slightly. Only thirty-seven psalms remained intact.

After some study and considerable discussion the committee decided to print the entire Psalter, realizing that some psalms and portions of others might not be read as part of a worship service. This was a congregation that had lived through two world wars, the wars in Korea and Vietnam, and the genocides in Europe, Africa, and Southeast Asia. They understood that the self-righteous wrath and violence of the psalms might warn a people against the passions and self-righteousness in their own time.

Realizing that the cadence, wording, and the imagery of the King James Version were important in public worship, the committee continued to print most psalms in that translation. In more than sixty instances, however, the committee thought the King James translation was unclear and used the Revised Standard Version. King's Chapel's affiliate minister, the Rev. Charles Forman, who taught Hebrew and Arabic at Wheaton College, guided the committee in this process.

The 150 psalms in the Psalter are divided into five sections: 1–41, 42–72, 73–89, 90–106, and 107 to 150. Each section ends with a doxology that begins "Blessed be the Lord God of Israel." The psalms in the first four sections show markedly different feelings and intentions. The fifth section contains mostly psalms of praise, trust, and thanksgiving with such exceptions as 130 and 137.

The psalms range widely in mood and intensity because the psalmists poured out their feelings without restraint as if they felt no shame before

God. We may be astonished at their fury, fear, grief, and despair, but it seems that the psalmists trusted God to understand, accept, and forgive them regardless of their passions. As "low" as the psalmists go, so "high" they also rise.

Think of all the moods in which we can pray the psalms:

>If we are fearful, we can plead.
>
>If we are angry, we can curse.
>
>If we are sad, we can weep.
>
>If we are joyful, we can exult.
>
>If we are hopeful, we can trust.
>
>If we are guilty, we can confess.
>
>If we are grateful, we can give thanks.
>
>If we feel stupid, we can be instructed.
>
>If we are desperate, we can ask for mercy.

The psalms are both song and poetry. No wonder John Calvin called the psalms "The anatomy of the soul, a mirror in which we can see ourselves."

Athanasius wrote, "The psalms become like a mirror to the one who sings them."

John Donne called the psalms "the manna of the church." Recently, Kathleen Norris wrote of her visit to a Benedictine monastery. "In singing the psalms with the monks," she said, "I felt as if I were becoming part of a living and lived-in poem."

Athanasius in the fourth century, John Donne in the seventeenth, Kathleen Norris in the twentieth, and the faithful for more than two millennia have said, read, sung, chanted, and prayed the psalms in churches, monasteries, cathedrals, and their homes.

Christians have sung the psalms in three ways—in unison as a chant or metrical hymn, responsively between choir or cantor singing the verses alternately, and antiphonally, the people singing a single verse (an antiphon) in response to the verses sung by choir or cantor.

The psalms have power because they are poetry, the most compact form of speech or writing. The poetry of the psalms lies not in rhyme, but in rhythm, balance, repetition, images, and disjunction.

Rhythm catches our attention and helps to fix the text in our memories. It is a key element in Hebrew and in good translations into other languages.

The lines in a psalm verse will vary in length, but they keep a pattern of beats. Often each line will have the same number of beats: "The Lord is my shepherd" and "I shall not want." (23:1)

Sometimes the first line will have one beat more than the second line: "The heavens declare the glory of God" and " The firmament showeth his handiwork."(19:1)

The above are only two examples of several rhythmic patterns used in the psalms.

Balance is also important. Each verse of a psalm has two, three, and sometimes four lines, making a single sentence. Regardless of the number of lines in a verse, they are balanced to form two contrasting or harmonizing thoughts. For example, the second line may restate the thought in the first line: "To thee, O Lord, I cried, And to the Lord I made supplication." (30:8)

The second line may complete the first thought: "The law of the Lord is perfect, converting the soul. The testimony of the Lord is sure, making wise the simple." (19:7)

The second line might contrast with the first: "The wicked borrow and do not pay back, But the righteous are generous and keep giving." (37:21)

Repetition can reinforce a particular message as in Psalm 136 where the second line of all twenty-six verses is "For his mercy endureth forever." A line may be repeated only once as in Psalm 129, which begins, "Often have they afflicted me from my youth, let Israel now say, often have they afflicted me from my youth." By repeating a line the psalmist is telling us, "I really want you to remember this."

Images abound in the psalms—green pastures, still waters, dark valleys, a parched deer panting for cool water, a wise man standing like a well-planted tree, a soul calmed like a child at its mother's breast, or the God who turns our mourning into dancing. Sometimes the image is subtle as in Psalm 1, which begins "Blessed is the man who walks not in the counsel of the ungodly, nor stands in the way of sinners, nor sits in the seat of the scornful." Sometimes the image hits us right in the face as in "Shuddering seized them, their pain like a woman in labor." (Psalm 48:6)

Disjunction produces surprise in poetry. Although many psalms maintain a consistent mood throughout—trust in Psalm 23, praise in Psalm 118, or gratitude in Psalm 136—others make startling changes. The voice may go from the first person to third without warning. The speaker may shift without explanation from the psalmist to the listener to God. The mood may change from soulful longing to violent fury, as in Psalm 137, which asks "How shall we sing the Lord's song in a strange land?" but ends with "O daughter of Babylon, ... happy shall he be who takes your little ones and dashes them against the rocks." Or the shift may go in the other direction; after boasting about how much he hates his enemies, the psalmist in 139 ends by praying, "Search me, O God, and know my heart! Try me and know my heart! And see if there be any wicked way in me, and lead me in the way everlasting."

Even today, the psalms are truly "the manna of the church." They represent to us the age-old themes of sin, sorrow, anger, guilt, judgment, grace, joy, and thanksgiving. They tell us who we are before God and who God is among us.

The psalms are inexhaustible. Over the centuries they have often been the church's strongest prayers. They speak to us and often for us better than we can speak to or for ourselves. We can read and consider them in small portions slowly and thoughtfully in the process called *lectio divina*. When we memorize such psalms as 30, 130, or 131, they become our own prayers.

For this reason many congregations still sing or say several psalms during the course of a Sunday service. Psalms may be sung to simple plainsong settings, or to the many new settings such as simplified plainsong or the lush settings of the French priest and composer Joseph Gelineau (1920 – 2008) or those of the Taize community.

The Sermon

Congregations have a right to expect from a sermon the Word of God spoken to the changing fortunes of their lives. They want instruction, inspiration, and guidance. The preacher has at his or her disposal three means of satisfying the congregation's expectations.

First is the range of texts available. For centuries preachers had to deal with the same Epistle and Gospel texts every year in Catholic, Orthodox, and Episcopalian churches. The Second Vatican Council produced a three-year lectionary enabling the people to hear and the priest to consider a much wider range of readings from the Old Testament, the Epistles, and Gospels. Subsequent lectionaries have maintained this rich variety.

Second is the preacher's preparation. He or she should preach not so much on the text as off the text. It should provide the platform from which the sermon is launched and the guidance system that directs its trajectory. The preacher's exploration of the text will lead to discovering the trajectory for a particular sermon addressed to a particular people at a particular time. The people need to hear the preacher deal with the reality of their personal and public lives, but from a perspective they don't find elsewhere. The preacher may speak on political events, public crises, personal fulfillment, or theological matters, as Boston preachers often did in the seventeenth and eighteenth centuries. These are age-old concerns for which the Bible provides wisdom. The preacher's task is to discover and interpret this wisdom.

Finally there is the matter of the placement of the sermon in the service. When the sermon comes at the end, it may become the highlight of worship and the congregation may need to be reminded of the lessons. When the sermon follows immediately the reading of the lessons, as in Holy Communion, the explication of the text is a natural action and the wisdom of scripture more apparent. The sermon is part of the liturgy, not its culmination.

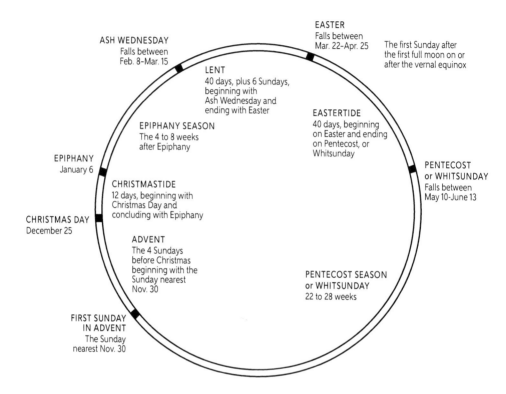

This image was designed for the 1986 edition of the King's Chapel *Book of Common Prayer*. Please read it clockwise, beginning with the First Sunday in Advent, found in the lower left of the circle.

THE CHRISTIAN YEAR

———————✠———————

Christianity is not just a collection of teachings, worship services, or organizations. It is also a calendar, a way of setting the mystery of time into a certain order. We live according to several calendars—fiscal, academic, seasonal, and sports.

The Christian calendar sets our Sundays and holy days into an order that helps us relive the events through which God has disclosed himself to us. Through these re-enactments of God's self-disclosure we discover God's judgment, grace, commands, and the future God has promised to us. The Christian calendar marks these days with specific chants, hymns, prayers, scripture readings, customs, and liturgical traditions.

The first half of the Christian year, lasting five to six months, is divided into five seasons: Advent, Christmas, Epiphany, Lent, and Easter, and covers the anticipation, birth, ministry, Passion, and resurrection of Jesus. The second half of the year, Pentecost, six to seven months long, is a single season and covers the life of the holy Spirit in the new church and the church's reenactment of Christ's ministry and God's kingdom.

Our prayer book includes services for only three of the feast days, Christmas Eve, Good Friday, and the Easter Vigil, as well as the Welcome for New Members.

Sunday

The most frequently celebrated day in the church year is not an annual festival but the weekly celebration that takes place on what was in the first century and still is the first day of the week. "On the first day of the week"

St. Paul and the Christians of Troas gathered to "break bread" according to Acts 20:7. St. Paul enjoins the Christians in Corinth to put aside whatever they intend to give to the church, "on the first day of every week." (I Corinthians 16:2)

The first day of the week was not a day of rest, but a working day in the Mediterranean world. Therefore, Christians gathered early on Sunday morning for a brief Eucharist before going to work. They also gathered the night before for an extended vigil service.

Christians called Sunday "the day of the Lord." The inspired author of Revelation writes in 1:10, "On the Lord's day I was in the spirit." The Day of the Lord became *Domenica* in Latin, a name preserved in current romance languages. The English name for this day hearkens back to its old pagan name, *dies solis*, the day of the sun.

Not until 321 CE, when the emperor Constantine forbade work on that day, did "the Day of the Lord" become a new Sabbath, thus making the Jewish Sabbath a work day. Over the centuries the prohibition of work on Sundays extended to sports, games, plays, buying, selling, idle conversation, and almost any pleasurable activity. In our time, despite weekends away, soccer and hockey practice, home chores, and the opening of virtually all retail enterprises, this day remains the central day for Christian worship. The Second Vatican Council permitted celebrations of the Sunday Eucharist on Saturday evening.

Advent

At its outset as throughout the year the Christian calendar runs in serious counterpoint to other calendars. For Christians the four weeks in Advent (six in Orthodox churches) are a time of looking forward to something better than the chaos of history and the exhausting preparations for Christmas. In church Christians hear the prophets' promises and the warnings of John the Baptist. They sing the age-old songs of longing, and they pray for the approach of One who says to us, "Come to me, all you who are weary and heavy-burdened, and I will give you rest." (Matthew 11:28)

During Advent, Orthodox Christians fast and attend evening services, as they do in Lent. Thus, they call this season "Small Lent." The purpose of these disciplines is not to suffer or prove oneself, but to open oneself to God's presence.

Christmas Eve

In 1910 King's Chapel began to hold services on Christmas Eve. In 1989 it instituted a service of lessons and carols, begun in 1880 at Truro Cathedral in England. This service was popularized by its celebration at King's College, Cambridge. The service consists of eight lessons, interspersed with carols that tell the story of our salvation including creation, fall, and prophecy, then the annunciation and the birth of Jesus, as well as his ministry and the mystery of the incarnation.

Christmas

The big question Christmas asks is, "What are we celebrating?" The obvious answer is: the birth of Jesus; therefore the two big celebrations are the children's nativity pageant and the choir's Christmas Eve service. At both services people who might otherwise have never come to church are glad to be there. Everyone's theological guard is down. The children's reenactment of Jesus' birth and the lovely carols and anthems are enough to warm the most indifferent heart. The infant Jesus is everyone's infant, and thus no threat to anyone.

But why is the birth of Jesus important? And who is this Jesus whose birth we celebrate? A teacher? A reformer? A good example? A hero? A god? The church's answer is: All these, yes, but much more. God, yes, but not a god, not one god among the many gods of the spiritual and secular marketplace. This infant is an intruder into history, God's own Word, who comes disguised in our fragile and mortal flesh.

Here lies the heart of Christian faith. The Word that God spoke at creation, and spoke again through the Law, and spoke yet again through the prophets, and once again through the teachers of wisdom—this Word, once only spoken, now was lived. This Word became our flesh and our blood in an unknown and unlikely stranger from a rustic province in a conquered land. In a carpenter, God brought us a kingdom that is always beginning and will someday come in completion.

The early Christians had little or no interest in Christ's birth compared to his death, resurrection, ascension, and eventual return. But, as time passed and his return was delayed, the church took more interest in the birth stories, and by the middle 300s was beginning to celebrate Christ's birth on December 25, the former pagan festival of *sol invictus*, the day of the unconquered sun.

The Puritans in England and the Massachusetts Bay Colony, mindful of its pagan origins, ignored Christmas. King's Chapel was the first church in New England to observe the day. The congregation decked their newly built sanctuary with greens and celebrated Holy Communion, much to the displeasure of Boston's Puritan citizens. Except for a twenty-five year hiatus (1963–1989) King's Chapel has celebrated Holy Communion on Christmas morning and taken up a collection for the poor. Often the congregation has been small. Never has it been disappointed.

The Twelve Days of Christmas

The days after Christmas are sober occasions. December 26th is the feast day of St. Stephen, the first Christian martyr. The 27th is the feast day of St. John the Divine who attacked Rome as the beast in the book of Revelation. The reading for December 28th describes Herod's massacre of the infants in Bethlehem. The 29th is devoted to Thomas Becket, the martyred bishop of Canterbury. The last two days of December are devoted to early Christian martyrs. In this way Christmas points toward the crucifixion.

Epiphany

January 6, coming twelve days after Christmas, was observed in the Eastern church as early as the year 200 and marked the baptism of Christ in the Jordan. It also celebrated the manifestation (the Greek word is *epiphanios*) of Christ as the Incarnation of God's Word.

In the Western church this feast day took on another meaning. The church in Rome celebrated it as Christ's manifestation to the non-Jewish world, symbolized by the three magi who came to be represented as kings. Their gifts symbolized the three roles of Christ: gold for kingship, frankincense for priesthood, and myrrh (a spice used in embalming) for sacrifice.

Lent

Lent began as only a two-to-three day period of fasting and prayer before Easter. Records of a forty-day fast are dated around the year 325. The number forty is based on the years of the Hebrew tribes in the desert, Elijah's sojourn on Mt. Horeb, and Christ's sojourn in the wilderness. The forty-day Lent soon became the norm in the West.

Fasting meant abstention from wine, oil, meat, and fish. In the West the discipline of fasting has been mitigated almost to the point of extinction. The Eastern churches still take it seriously.

Lent was originally an occasion for public and severe penance for egregious sinners. Those under the ban of excommunication stood at the church door with ashes scattered over their heads, asking those who entered to pray for their reinstatement in the church.

Lent was the time for candidates to prepare for their baptism on Easter. These candidates were and still are called catechumens, from the Greek word *catacheo*, meaning "to teach." During Lent, catechumens as well as baptized Christians attended Sunday and weekday services where they heard preachers explaining the scriptures and teaching the basic doctrines of the church. Catechumens were dismissed after the sermon, not to be present at communion until baptized.

We now have English translations of these Lenten sermons, especially those of St. Augustine, bishop of Hippo in North Africa, and of St. John Chrysostom, bishop of Constantinople.

Ash Wednesday

Lent became a season of penitence. Every Christian was expected to be in church on the first day of Lent for the imposition of ashes made from the burnt palms of last year's Passion (Palm) Sunday. Then as now the priest said to each penitent, "Remember that you are dust and to dust you shall return," while he used the ashes to mark their foreheads in the sign of the cross. The scripture lesson for this day is the temptation of Christ in the desert.

From its founding, King's Chapel held Morning Prayer on Ash Wednesday, but there was no imposition of ashes until the arrival of the Rev. Joseph Barth in 1955. A rational and thoughtful Unitarian, he was raised Catholic and brought this ancient practice to our congregation. It continues to this day.

The Eastern Lent of seven weeks begins, not with the imposition of ashes, but with a rite of mutual forgiveness held after the morning liturgy. The Orthodox calendar calls this Forgiveness Sunday.

Palm Sunday

There are two ways to celebrate this last Sunday in Lent. The minister may read the account of Jesus' entry into Jerusalem and preach upon this text. Or members of the congregation, taking the role of Jesus, Pilate, etc., read the account of Jesus' Passion. In either case the congregation will sing verses of a hymn describing Christ's triumphal entry into Jerusalem, while the children of the parish pass out palms.

The undistributed palms are saved and burnt on the morning of the next year's Ash Wednesday and distributed at the noonday service.

Maundy Thursday

The name of this day has a history. St. John, the author of the fourth Gospel, must have heard at least one of the Gospel accounts that describes how Jesus ate the Last Supper with his disciples. But instead of describing that meal as the other Gospels do, St. John describes how Jesus washed his disciples' feet. Then Jesus says, "I have given you an example that you should do as I have done to you … I give you a new commandment that you love one another, even as I have loved you. By this all will know that you are my disciples, if you love one another." (John 13:15, 34-35)

Peter objects to his master washing his feet, but Jesus says, "If I do not wash you, you have no part in me." Jesus' message is clear. Whoever follows him must first receive his love, which is embodied not in words but in an act of physical service. Only those who accept God's love will be able to share it with others. No disciple can give without receiving.

Jesus' words are a command, and the Latin word for "command" is *mandatum*. Maundy is the English contraction of the Latin *mandatum*. During the first Maundy Thursday services, held in the fourth century, the clergy washed the feet of certain members of the parish.

The first King's Chapel prayer books printed only a prayer and a lesson for this day, but by 1910 King's Chapel was holding a communion service. After the service the minister and assistants stripped the chancel of everything except the communion table itself in preparation for the stark services on Good Friday. Some years ago we instituted the washing of feet.

Good Friday

This day is known by different names in different countries. It may be called Long Friday, Great Friday, Holy Friday, or Sorrowful Friday, but we call it Good Friday and for good reason.

It is Good Friday because Christ was not simply a passive victim. Yes, he died a painful death and we hear that described in brief, clear detail. The Gospels tell us, however, that Jesus actively sought his death in order to break into hell, the realm of death itself. The Orthodox icon for *Pascha*/Easter shows Jesus, not coming out of the tomb, but standing in hell and lifting Adam and Eve out of the grave. Why? Because God through Jesus assaults the realm of death itself and rescues the souls who are perishing there. In hell, Jesus, the victim, becomes Jesus, the victor. Terrible as his death was, it brought new life into this world, and therefore we contemplate it with solemn gratitude.

The early church saw Good Friday as part of a single event, a three-day cycle called the *Triduum*, beginning with the crucifixion and ending in the resurrection. The first and third days did not oppose each other but stood together as parts of God's single plan for our redemption.

Many have witnessed to the power of Good Friday. Julian of Norwich (1342–1416) contemplated the crucifixion in a series of sixteen visions, and out of that experience wrote a powerful testimony to God's love in her *Revelations of Divine Love*. Edith Sitwell (1887–1964) mourned our violence and saw God's love in a Good Friday elegy titled, "Still falls the rain." Sydney Carter (1915–2004) in his fine, ironic poem, "Good Friday" testified to God's death on the cross and, implicitly, to our redemption. A once agnostic friend began her journey to conversion at a Good Friday service. Perhaps Dietrich Bonhoeffer (1906-1945) summed it up in his last words before his execution: "This is the end; for me the beginning."

Some churches hold a traditional three-hour service during which short sermons are preached on the seven last words of Jesus. Other churches hold an evening service when the Passion story is read, interspersed with psalms and chants. During this reading and chanting the church is slowly darkened. Orthodox congregations, like their predecessors in the fourth century, hear all four Gospel accounts of the Passion as well as psalms, Epistles and prophets on Good Friday.

For most of King's Chapel's first three centuries the priest read Morning Prayer and preached a sermon on this day. In the 1800s the morning service became a noon service, as it is now. About a hundred years ago the minister added a 5:00 p.m. service, perhaps for those going home from work.

When the Reverend Joseph Barth came to King's Chapel in 1955, he instituted an evening service called *Tenebrae*. The original service of *Tenebrae*, (the word means "darkness") combined the morning offices for Maundy Thursday, Good Friday and Holy Saturday, taking psalms, chants, and prayers from each.

At one point King's Chapel had three Good Friday services, held at noon, 5:00 p.m., and 8:00 p.m.. Given the low attendance at the 5:00 p.m. service, it was dropped. The 8:00 p.m. service, a revised *Tenebrae*, is now a reading of the Passion story, interspersed with antiphons and responses between the minister and choir. The church is lit with candles, which are gradually extinguished as the service progresses. The service ends with the Lord's Prayer, an abrupt closing of the Bible with the sound of finality, and the slow procession of the Christ candle down the center aisle and out of the darkened church.

Although the entire service is not printed here, one prayer is worthy of inclusion:

Almighty God, whose most dear Son went not up to joy but first he suffered pain, and entered not into glory before he was crucified, mercifully grant that we, walking in the way of the cross, may find it to be none other than the way of life and peace; through the same Jesus Christ our Lord. *Amen.*

The Easter or Paschal Vigil

It would make no sense to discuss the Easter services without speaking of that stunning and inexplicable explosion that we call the resurrection. Without this there would be nothing that we could call Christian.

It would also make no sense to try to explain the mystery of this explosion. For at its center stands a being so like and so unlike us, a death-breaker, a sin-scorner, who time and again in history and in our time has re-appeared out of every grave that culture, academia, and the church itself have dug for him.

Suffice it to say that Christian faith began with the experience of Christ's first followers. They believed the man whom they saw die on a cross lived among them as a this-and-other-worldly being as well as one who gave them power to witness to his kingdom. The baffling resurrection narratives, therefore, describe an incarnate being, both flesh and spirit, human and divine.

The Gospels tell us that not everyone believed the resurrection. "Some doubted," says Matthew 28:17. Mary, the disciples, and the travelers on the road to Emmaus at first did not recognize the risen Christ. When St. Paul preached to the Athenians on the resurrection, some of them ridiculed him, and others said, "We'll hear you later on this." St. Paul reports that Jews and Greeks alike considered the resurrection to be foolishness. (I Corinthians 1:22)

One thing is clear. What seemed to be the end of Jesus was the beginning. The "Last" Supper was replaced by an evening meal at an inn in Emmaus where two travelers recognized Jesus when he took, blessed, and broke bread with them. The new era was also heralded by a lakeside breakfast, at which this worldly-and-other-worldly Jesus ate with his disciples in Galilee. His seven "last" words on the cross were replaced by new words, "Peace be with you," (John 20:19) "Do not be afraid," (Matthew 28:10) and "Lo, I am with you always." (Matthew 28:17)

As Christians we are called into the company of this resurrection, and though we don't always know what we're doing, we still praise, pray, preach, sing, and in our liturgies enact the mystery that is the heart of our hope. That is why we call Pascha/Easter the day of days, the feast of feasts, the sabbath of all sabbaths.

Most English-speaking Christians call it Easter, a name of English origin. The church historian Bede (673–735) reports that it came from the name of an Anglo-Saxon spring goddess, *Eostre*.

Presently most Christians, like the first Christians, call this day Pascha, Greek for the Hebrew *pesach* which means "a passing over." For, this day marks our Passover, our slow and often tardy passing out of the realm of this world's gods into the world of the one, true God. The Easter hymn, "Come, ye faithful, raise the strain," expresses this theology with elegant clarity.

At first every Sunday, a working day, was the day of resurrection for the first Christians. But the first three Gospels report Christ's crucifixion on a specific day of the year, namely the day after the Jewish Passover, and his resurrection on the first day of the next week. Therefore it was only a matter of time before Christian bishops and churches created an annual observance of the resurrection. After some debate, the council of bishops' meeting at Nicea in 325 CE determined that Easter/Pascha should fall on the first Sunday after the first full moon after the spring equinox, which means it can take place on any day between March 21 and April 25. A small group of Christians still celebrate the day according to the Jewish lunar calendar.

Currently, there are two principal Easter services among Western churches—the Vigil on the evening before Easter Sunday and the Sunday morning celebration.

The first Christians held a vigil service on the evening before every Sunday. In time the vigil preceding Easter/Pascha became the single celebration. The current ceremony is a somewhat shortened version of the earlier services.

After prayers of preparation, the Vigil begins with the procession of the Christ candle into a darkened church and as the congregation sings the whole church is illuminated. There follows the reading of seven to twelve lessons telling the story of our salvation beginning with creation, fall, exodus, and Passover, continuing with the prophecies from Isaiah and others, and culminating in the ministry, sacrifice, and resurrection of Christ. Portions of Psalm 118 are read between these lessons.

There follow baptisms and the renewal of baptismal vows and then the celebration of the Eucharist. In all Eastern churches and some Western churches the brief and brilliant paschal sermon of St. John Chrysostom is read.

King's Chapel adopted this service in 1972, in part because Holy Communion had not been celebrated on Easter for more than twenty years. There was also a sense that the resurrection needed a more distinctive and convincing celebration than the usual service of Morning Prayer on Easter Sunday. Our present prayer book provides a bare outline of the Easter Vigil, but its celebration requires, and now has, a service book of its own.

Easter Sunday

Easter Sunday is a day of happy celebration. Churches are packed, flowers abound, triumphant hymns and grand anthems are sung, the sermon is upbeat, smiles are everywhere as is Easter finery.

King's Chapel celebrated Holy Communion on Easter Sunday until 1952 when the vestry voted to drop that service and substitute Morning Prayer in its place. But in 2015 the new minister, the Rev. Joy Fallon, wisely re-instituted the celebration of Holy Communion.

By 1910 King's Chapel was holding an additional service on the afternoon of Easter Sunday in which children in the church school were promoted to the next rank and given flowers. By 1967 this celebration was so poorly attended that it was discontinued. Children now receive their Easter flowers at the end of the morning service.

The reader might be interested to know that the first chancel drama took place on an Easter Sunday in about the year 900. A white-robed priest, representing an angel, sat by a curtained tomb. Three priests representing the three Marys approached him. The angel priest asked, "Whom do you seek, followers of Christ?" The three answered, "Jesus of Nazareth, O dweller in heaven." At this the angel priest ripped the curtain off the tomb, revealing a cross, representing Christ, and said, "He is not here, but is risen. Go and announce that he is risen from the tomb." The three priests sang, "The Lord is risen," as the cathedral bells began to ring and the choir sang, "Alleluia."

The Reformation churches abolished this kind of drama, but the trade guilds in England took it up and developed the annual mystery and miracle plays dramatizing such Bible stories as Noah and the Flood and the birth of Christ.

Pentecost

We can never understand the reality of the holy Spirit as long as we think of it as a spiritual faculty, ability, or gift that some people have and others don't. The holy Spirit is not just the possession of individuals, but of the whole community of faith. It is not only a personal inspiration, but a revelation to the whole church, and this is clear from the account in Acts 2 where the one hundred and twenty apostles, including the twelve disciples, had gathered in one place. This company was not a collection of individuals but the church-to-be.

The account in Acts 2 reports the mystery of the holy Spirit's visitation as, first, a sound, like a rushing wind, and then lights, like tongues of flame, resting on the heads of the twelve, who begin to speak in at least fifteen of the languages known in the Mediterranean world. The twice-repeated word "like" tells us that the words "wind" and "lights" are attempts to suggest an indescribable power that can be known only by its effects.

For what is the effect of the inrushing of "holy Spirit?" Expression! Communication! The apostles speak and not just to each other, but to the known world, which is represented by the visitors to Jerusalem who are watching and hearing this astonishing event. In Peter's sermon (see Acts 2:14-36) we see this uncontrollable drive to speak as he rebuts the charge of onlookers that the inspired company is drunk with new wine.

The book of Acts then describes the travels, adventures, and sermons of missionaries like Peter, Paul, Barnabas, Timothy, and Silvanus. Their gift of preaching and organizing increases not only the number of converts, but also the range of gifts that an expanding church will need in order to survive—witnessing, healing, teaching, administration, pastoral care, and generosity. St. Paul describes these gifts in I Corinthians 12. Thus the church grows.

All this is the effect of what happened on the first Pentecost and what has happened since. A Spanish nun named Egeria visited Jerusalem in the year 385 and left us with her report of a day-long series of liturgies on Pentecost in that city. Soon Pentecost was second only to Easter in importance, and like Easter, it became the occasion for baptisms and had its own readings, chants, and prayers.

The name, Pentecost, from the Greek word for fifty, describes the interval between this day and Pascha/Easter, just as the Jewish harvest festival, *Shavuot*, follows Passover by the same number of days.

In England Pentecost is also known as Whitsunday, possibly because candidates for baptisms and confirmations usually wore white. Some suggest that "Whit" stands for "wit," a synonym for the wisdom given to the apostles on that day.

Recently churches have begun to realize the rich meanings inherent in this festival. Some congregations read the lesson from Acts 2 in several languages. Some congregations recite the Lord's Prayer simultaneously or sequentially in several tongues. Still others in place of a sermon offer chancel drama or other enactments, depicting the power of the holy Spirit.

All Saints and All Souls Sunday

This day honors both the lesser saints and the many souls who have served the church well.

During the church's first three centuries many Christians died in the intermittent persecutions visited upon them by local mobs, provincial rulers, or emperors in Rome. These men and women were called martyrs, a legal term that originally described a witness in a court case. Christians came to see their persecutions as a trial, a test of their loyalty. A martyr, therefore, was a witness to the God of Jesus Christ.

The first martyr in Christian history was Stephen, a deacon whose death is described in Acts 7:54-60. He was followed by such well-known martyrs as Polycarp, bishop of Smyrna, Justin, a theologian in Rome, and Cyprian, bishop of Antioch. Thousands followed in their train, many with a day in the church calendar assigned to their remembrance and veneration.

But soon there were too many martyrs for each to be honored with a special day and mass. By the time of St. John Chrysostom (347–407 CE) congregations in the East remembered these lesser-known martyrs at a mass on the Sunday after Pentecost. In Rome Pope Boniface IV rededicated the Pantheon in the year 609 as the church of Saint Mary and the Martyrs and set May 13 as the day for their memorial mass. Gregory III moved that celebration to a chapel in the Vatican and the date to November 1, which remains All Saints Day in the Christian calendar.

Many Christians, of course, did not die for their faith, but lived sacrificial lives. In the year 998, St. Odilio, abbot of the Cistercian monastery in Cluny, France, held a mass in memory of these Christians. This custom spread to other churches, and eventually November 2, assigned as the day for their remembrance, became All Souls Day.

Since November 1 and 2 usually fall on weekdays, and since few parishioners were likely to attend weekday services, King's Chapel began in 1986 to celebrate All Saints and All Souls Sunday on the first Sunday of November. We read lessons, say prayers and sing hymns appropriate to the occasion. We invite friends and family members of those who have died since the last year's service to enter the chancel and light a candle in memory of their loved one.

The rich history of the prayer book and its fine
language may lend comfort and insight and invite
God's presence wherever one opens it.

YOUR PERSONAL PRAYER BOOK

———————✖———————

The prayer book serves not only congregations. It is also a manual of personal devotion. Francis Greenwood intended that his 1828 edition be such a book when he wrote, "May this volume be found worthy to be taken to the worshiper's home, to go with the traveller on his journey, and the sailor on the sea." The present prayer book can serve as such a manual in the following ways.

On pages 153 through 182, the reader will find prayers to be said at morning, evening, work, meals, and bedtime. There are prayers for those in sickness, guilt, and discouragement, for the sleepless and the traveller, and even for the concertgoer. One could also say the Lord's Prayer, the Jesus Prayer, the Hail Mary, or other memorable devotions.

On pages 273 through 477, the reader will find the complete Psalter. Pages 479 through 529 have a two-year lectionary with Old Testament, Epistle and Gospel readings for each day of the week.

When you use a text, feel free to make that text your own. If you wish, put some or all of it in your own words. If you are saying a psalm, you may want to leave out some parts of it. Or you might rephrase those in your own words. Remember these are your prayers. Say them as they speak to you. Forget what anyone else might think.

If you find that certain prayers, psalms, poems, or scripture readings become important to you, you might memorize them. Then they become yours. You can say them whenever you want to. And if you don't remember them completely, that does not matter. God's presence, not your perfection, is what you need.

In reading the psalms, you might start with the short ones, such as Psalm 42, Psalm 121, Psalm 139, or the favorite of so many, Psalm 23. When you read them, you might read them aloud to yourself, just as you may when you read your favorite poems. In so doing the psalms, and poems, will become more real to you.

One can pray by singing familiar hymns or chants, or by reading or reciting passages of scripture, special poems, or passages of prose. One may remember friends, family, neighbors, or public concerns. One can also pray by writing in a spiritual journal, by prayerful walking, meditating, or doing yoga or tai chi.

One woman told her priest that she had been saying the Jesus Prayer for fourteen years and never felt God's presence. The priest told her to forget the Jesus Prayer, sit in her chair and knit for fifteen minutes, occasionally looking around and noticing what was in the room. She did so, hearing only the ticking of the clock and the click of her knitting needles. As the days passed she felt not only God's presence but gratitude for the lovely place she lived in.

Above all we must remember that when we are alone with God there is no one way or right way to say what we need that day. We must follow the inclination of our hearts that day, namely, the direction of the holy Spirit. This may differ from day to day. Sometimes we may not read scripture or pray for others. Sometimes we may simply sit in silence. If we follow the heart, the heart will tell us how to receive our "daily bread."

A final word: less is more. Do not try to overdo your practice. Do not try to keep an over-regimented devotional schedule. A few moments in God's presence (and you may not feel that every day) are enough. Let the Spirit guide you.

If you would like a copy of the King's Chapel prayer book for these purposes, we suggest that you inquire at admin@kings-chapel.org.

The Reverend Francis William Pitt Greenwood, seen here in a portrait that hangs in King's Chapel's parish house, edited revisions of the prayer book in 1828, 1831, and 1841. Such gradual changes in the prayer book keep it fresh for each new generation.

THE FUTURE OF THE PRAYER BOOK

————————✠————————

Does the prayer book have a future? One could say "No" for many reasons. Is not the membership of prayer book churches declining? Do not many already use handouts instead of a book? Will paper itself survive in a digital era? Will common prayer have a place in a culture of rampant individualism? Is not this commentary itself already an anachronism?

This guide is based on an assumption that prayer book worship will survive. This will happen, however, only if those who worship through the prayer book experience the life, energy, and hope that Christians have experienced in the past.

How might this happen? The usual answer in our day is to revise the text. As the reader has seen in the history section of this guide, prayer books go through periodic revision, some enduring and some as transient as the word "modern." Yet it is certain that if the prayer book text does not evolve, it will either die or become a museum piece. We can trust neither the literalists who believe that liturgies never change nor the modernists who press for constant change and believe that revision will lead to popular success.

The success of revision depends on the knowledge, wisdom, and faith of the revisers, and on the calm, deliberate, but unpressured pace of the revision process. As we saw from the 1925 revision of the King's Chapel prayer book, haste and anxiety produced little change and much irritation. The 1986 revision committee took more than five years to produce a book with many significant changes. In time another revision will take its place. Textual revision is part of liturgical evolution.

But a text is only part, and not the most important part, of a worship experience. For, what is worship? It is the enactment by clergy and congregation of the Bible's divine and human story of our creation, fall, judgment, restoration, and future. This enactment, which we earlier likened to a play, involves text, speech, song, movement, place, and space. The aim of such worship is to enable those who enact this liturgy to see that their own lives are told and retold in the great mega-story of God's encounter with our humankind.

Given the importance of text, let us consider how it might be enacted, beginning with speech. Anyone who is going to preach or lead worship needs serious training in interpreting a text to a congregation. An audible, articulate reader who interprets a text with appropriate inflection can make the weekly prayers or an annual Bible reading come alive in a moving and memorable way. No microphone or loudspeaker will make this happen, only training and practice. If seminaries required their students to take three years of voice lessons, they could produce amazing worship leaders.

Just as important, however, as the speaking of the clergy is the singing of the people, especially in prayer book churches. The people can sing three chants and three hymns, perhaps versicles and responses as well. We know how healing and energizing singing can be. We also know how dreadful it can be. What makes the difference?

First of all, simple words rich with images and reflecting the great biblical themes. Second, music that is singable and, if unfamiliar, carefully taught. Above all it takes clergy and music directors who realize that the congregation is the first choir. Of course there will and must be selected choirs of professionals and volunteers to provide soul-stirring music to move the people's hearts. That will stay in their minds. But what the people sing will inhabit their souls. The congregation may not remember what the preacher said by Sunday afternoon. But give them a great closing hymn and they will sing it for the rest of the week. And they'll be back the next Sunday.

The third feature of good liturgy is movement. Movement is essential to the enactment of story, and here we must speak of pews. For almost fifteen centuries the Christian church survived and flourished without pews. During the mass the faithful stood in the body (the nave) of the church. The aged and infirm sat in benches along the side and at the rear of the nave. But with the Reformation and the subsequent extended readings, prayers, and sermons, came first benches and then pews. What was the result?

First, the congregation was divided into the privileged, who sat near the preacher, and everyone else, who sat farther back. The pews also divided people from each other. They settled into space they imagined was their own possession. They worshipped God as a collection of families and individuals.

Pews gave people a sense that they were more the audience than the actors and actresses in this divine-and-human drama. In pew-bound worship, the choir's anthems and the sermon were the high point of the service. The churches deemed most successful provided the best spiritual entertainment. The others struggled and/or failed because they could not compete with sports, rock concerts, sitcoms, media games, or successful churches. They aimed for what they could never achieve.

Finally, pews imprisoned people. They made it difficult, at best inconvenient, to move. Small wonder that many of them wanted no part in processions and were glad to have communion brought to them.

The author realizes that this will make few, if any, converts. Congregations are loathe to abandon a four-century-old tradition of liturgical condominiums. But the reader is invited imaginatively to enter a church devoid of pews. And what is there? Space, empty space, holy space, space waiting for the people and priests to celebrate God's presence in ways they never thought of before.

In this imagined church there is space for movement: space for simple processions on festive days, space for members to bless one another as they return from communion, and space to gather around a child to be baptized, a couple to be married, or the casket of a loved one to be buried. There is space for small and special shrines dedicated, if only for a day, to holy people, holy causes, holy days in the church's year, but above all space for the people to experience each other as one congregation.

Recently some congregations provide movable chairs in their sanctuary in place of pews. This allows that space to be configured as desired.

And for the aged, the infirm, and the reluctant, as in the ancient days, there will always be space for them to be seated.

Now, what does space have to do with the prayer book?

Everything. Just as there can be space in the sanctuary, so can there be space in the liturgy, spaces between the paragraphs of prayers, psalms, and chants, and therefore opportunities for movement, music, and improvisation. All this can take place without altering the text of the liturgy. In fact, such improvisation supports, illustrates, and embellishes the text. Without some space between the notes all music would be noise, and so with words as well. All this is an unrealized part of a prayer book's evolution.

Space and movement may be the most radical means we have for enriching and interpreting the life within the text of the prayer book. How much better will future revisions be when the revisers know they are shaping a text for members of a congregation that worship with their bodies as well as with their lips and minds.

A final word to the reader. The last sixty years of the church's history have been a time of growth and decline, magnificence and triviality, martyrdom and betrayal, faithfulness and corruption. The faith once delivered to the saints has often been lost to the gods of this world. Yet that same faith has produced new saints and witnesses who refresh the church with their sacrifices and dedication.

The great hope of the church has never been based on what it was or was not at any moment in its history. Its hope and future lie in the One who was and is both Word and flesh, and who lives in the church the same yesterday, today, and tomorrow.

To whatever extent we at King's Chapel have been faithful to that One, to that same extent we have been sustained in what has been and still is the reason for our being—the praise of God and the service of our neighbor. Our liturgy has been our guide and stay in this endeavor. That is why in the introduction to our present prayer book we wrote: "We are sometimes asked why we keep the prayer book. In fact, it is the prayer book that has kept us."

As an unordained minister, James Freeman first served as lay reader for King's Chapel after the Revolutionary War. He led his congregation into Unitarianism, a Christian tradition with a long history and with churches even now in England, Romania, Hungary, and the United States. Freeman's Unitarianism came from dissident Anglican priests whose liturgical revisions furnished him with a model for the prayer book changes that he made. Freeman's Unitarianism provided a new religion, reflecting many of the precepts upon which the new nation of the United States was based. This painting by an unknown artist hangs in King's Chapel's parish house.

KEY FIGURES

Andrewes, Lancelot (1555–1626)

Bishop successively of Chichester (1605), Ely (1609), and Winchester (1619), and a renowned preacher, he was largely responsible for translating the first five books and the historical books of the Old Testament from Hebrew into English for the King James Bible. T. S. Eliot took the lines, "A cold coming we had of it, etc.," from one of Andrewes's sermons to open his poem, "The Journey of the Magi." Andrewes wrote the prayer, "Blessed art thou, O Lord our God," found at the beginning of Evensong.

Arius (c. 250–336 CE)

Arius was a priest in Alexandria who taught that Jesus Christ was created by God and therefore subordinate to Him. Christ was therefore a semi-divine person, an emanation from the Father, and subject to Him. God was eternal and immutable. Christ was not. The then bishop of Alexandria demanded that Arius recant, but he and his supporters refused to do so.

This dispute concerned the Emperor Constantine. He wanted no religious disruptions in his newly-united empire. Therefore he invited the entire body of Christian bishops to the first ecumenical council of the Christian church at the city of Nicea in 325.

The assembled bishops made what became the classic statement of Christian theology on the nature of God and Christ. They declared that Jesus was God's eternal word in flesh and therefore co-eternal with the Father, as the Nicene Creed declares: "God from God, Light from Light, True God from True God."

Since Christ is of God, the Council held, that Christ as God's Word was also the agent of creation, as again the Creed says, "through whom all things were made." This recognition of Christ's divine equality with God expanded into the doctrine of the Trinity with the added recognition of God's holy Spirit as God's presence among his people. Given that consensus, the bishops declared Arius's teachings to be heretical.

Centuries later, the first Unitarians came to believe in a semi-divine Jesus, as Arius taught. Others followed the teachings of Faustus Socinus (1539–1604) who believed in the teachings and resurrection of Jesus, yet

KEY FIGURES

denied his divinity. James Freeman was a Socinian, and his introduction to the 1785 King's Chapel prayer book, reprinted in the 1986 edition, makes this clear.

Athanasius (c. 296–373)

An ardent opponent of Arius, Athanasius became bishop of Alexandria after the Council of Nicea and served from 325 to 336. He was the author and chief defender of the Christology voted at the Council of Nicea in 325. In his essay *De Incarnatione* he held that Christ was both fully human and at the same time the Word of God by which the world and universe were created. Furthermore, Athanasius held that Christ was of the same being or essence as God the Father. From this evolved the classic doctrine of the Trinity, which is the faith of orthodox Christianity today.

St. Augustine of Hippo (354–430)

Raised by a pagan father and a Christian mother, Augustine became a brilliant teacher of rhetoric in North Africa, his homeland. He enjoyed continuing success in Rome and eventually in the emperor's court at Milan where he became the court rhetorician. Baptized by Ambrose, bishop of Milan, at age thirty-three, Augustine left the court for his homeland and served as the bishop of Hippo for the last thirty years of his life. A prolific writer and preacher, he dictated the story of his conversion in *The Confessions*, which he wrote thirteen years after the event. It was the first autobiography in Western literature and remains a Christian classic.

The second prayer in the opening of the burial service, "Blessed God, who cares so for each one of us," may be found on the first page of *The Confessions*.

Barth, Joseph (1906 1988)

The twelfth minister of King's Chapel (1955–1965) grew up on a farm in Kansas and was raised Catholic. At the University of Chicago he decided to become a Unitarian minister. He served the Unitarian church in Miami, Florida, and was active in that city's political life. Although he never changed the text of the prayer book, he instituted important changes in the worship services. He introduced the Good Friday evening service, the distribution of ashes on Ash Wednesday, the sung response and procession of the offering on Sunday morning, and a service for welcoming new members. He was the first minister to face the congregation from behind the communion table while celebrating Holy Communion. Upon leaving King's Chapel, he served for five years as director of ministry at the Unitarian Universalist Association before retiring to his large farm in Maine, where he raised vast quantities of vegetables and bred day lilies.

Becket, Thomas (c. 1118–1170)
A favorite of Henry II, Becket became archbishop of Canterbury in 1154 and a year later the king's chancellor. His opposition to the king's taxation policies, however, and his demand that English bishops place loyalty to the pope over loyalty to the king occasioned Henry's anger. On December 29 four knights killed Becket in the cathedral at the foot of the stairs leading to the choir where he was heading to attend vespers. His death made Canterbury an important pilgrimage site then and to this day.

Benedict of Nursia (c. 480–550)
A hermit by the age of twenty, Benedict lived for some years in a cave near Subiaco, Italy, where a community of monks gathered around him. He and his followers moved in 525 to Monte Cassino where they built a monastery. Benedict founded a dozen other abbeys and compiled a guide for them, called *The Rule*, which is the authoritative text for Roman Catholic monastic orders in our day.

Bunyan, John (1936–)
Born and raised in Australia, Bunyan was educated and ordained to the priesthood in England. He returned to his native land to serve as a parish priest in Sydney until he retired in 2001. In his active retirement he has written and published prayers, hymns, and services, which have been collected in a number of volumes, many of which celebrate Australian

KEY FIGURES

history and culture. He was an invaluable consultant to the 1986 committee and contributed at least ten prayers to that edition.

Castellio, Sebastian (1515–1563)

A Protestant theologian who taught in Geneva and Basel, his condemnation of the execution of Michael Servetus for heresy caused him to break with the Protestant mainstream in Switzerland. His *De Haeriticis* remains an eloquent plea for religious toleration.

Chrysostom ("the golden-tongued"), St. John (347–407)

The brilliant preacher of Constantinople served as its bishop from 398 to 404. When he denounced the decisions and behavior of the empress Theodoxia, she banished him to an exile of perpetual travel. He died exhausted from his enforced wanderings. His last reported words were, "Glory be to God for all things."

Like many, if not most Christians of his day, he was an egregious anti-Semite. But he was also a man of faith. One of his paschal sermons is still read at the Easter Eve liturgy at Orthodox churches around the world, and at King's Chapel as well. As St. Paul reminds us, we hold our treasures in earthen vessels.

Clarke, Samuel (1675–1729)

Chaplain to Queen Anne and for the last twenty years of his life rector of St. James's Church, Piccadilly, Clarke was censured by the Church of England for his Arian views as expressed in *On the Scripture Doctrine of the Trinity* (1712.) Arian Anglicans, like Clarke, questioned the Trinity, emphasized the human capacity to do good, and believed that the Bible, if read with reason as well as faith, was a sufficient rule for Christian belief and practice.

The council of Anglican bishops abandoned its demand that Clarke repudiate his views when he promised to publish no more on this topic. He kept his word, but privately amended his own copy of the 1662 prayer book, altering all references to the Trinity. From this book comes the doxology in

KEY FIGURES

use at King's Chapel. For more on this topic, see Doxology in the Glossary. A copy of his privately amended prayer book resides in the British Museum.

Cranmer, Thomas (1489–1556)

Archbishop of Canterbury for more than twenty years, he was a friend and ally of Henry VIII and annulled two of his marriages. He was also a scholar who read Hebrew, Greek, Latin, German, French, and Italian. He was the genius behind the Church of England's 1549 and 1552 prayer books. Borrowing from Bishop Herrmann's and Luther's liturgical innovations in Germany, Cardinal Quinone's innovations in Spain, and other sources, he wove these materials into his inherited Catholic tradition, producing the impressive liturgy that survives to this day.

Cranmer's glory was short-lived. Upon coming to power in 1553, Mary Tudor sent him to the Tower and three years later burned him at the stake, as she did 300 other clergy who refused to acknowledge the supremacy of Rome.

Cyprian (died 258)

Born a pagan and trained as a rhetorician, he became a Christian and three years later was named bishop of his hometown, Carthage, in 248. In that same year, he left Carthage during the persecution of Christians instituted by the emperor Decius, but governed his diocese in absentia by letter. He returned in 251. When a plague awoke a wave of local fear and hatred of Christians, he stayed and defended his people, citing their charitable works on behalf of the city's populace. When the next emperor, Valerian, instituted a second persecution, Cyprian remained in the city and was beheaded in 258.

He wrote short essays on timely theological topics and many letters to friends, parishioners, and opponents. He believed that Christianity survives through the church, as seen in the following quotations: "Outside the church there is no salvation." "There is one God, one Christ, and one church." "He can no longer have God as a Father who does not have the church as his mother."

KEY FIGURES

Donne, John (c. 1573–1631)

At first a rising political star in English politics and the brilliant author of secular poems, Donne was ordained to the Anglican priesthood in 1615, and in 1621 became the Dean of St. Paul's Cathedral in London. His preaching drew crowds of worshipers to the cathedral, and his religious poems attracted many readers as they do today.

Erasmus, Desiderius (c. 1466–1536)

He was born, raised, and ordained to the priesthood in the Netherlands, but he left his homeland in 1495 and spent the rest of his life as a wandering scholar, studying, teaching, and writing in Paris, Oxford, Cambridge, Brussels, Italy, Basel, Vienna, Freiburg and again Basel, where he died. His need to write what he believed may have necessitated this peripatetic life, for he not only pleaded for religious freedom, but he also attacked the corruptions of the Catholic church with bitter satire and argued with such Protestants as Martin Luther. Although he was the most famous scholar in Europe, at his life's end he was vilified by Protestants and Catholics alike. In time, the world would profit by his example and by his translations of the New Testament and the works of the church fathers. His name remains an emblem of Christian humanism.

David, Francis (1510–1579)

Trained for the Catholic priesthood, he briefly became a Lutheran and then a Calvinist. He began to preach a Unitarian interpretation of Christianity after reading the works of Michael Servetus. David preached that God created his Son Jesus Christ and gave him his divinity, thus setting aside the doctrine of the Trinity. By his preaching and example, David founded the Unitarian church in Transylvania, which continues to this day in both Hungary and Romania. Under David's influence, the king of Transylvania, John Sigismund, allowed Catholic, Calvinist, Lutheran, and Unitarian churches to worship freely according to their own traditions, since he argued that "faith is the gift of God." Transylvania was the only country in Europe where this happened. John

KEY FIGURES

Sigismund's successor abandoned that example and put Francis David in the castle prison at Deva, where he died.

Forman, Charles (1920–1998)

Raised in the Nazarene Church, he explored other church traditions as an adolescent and became a Unitarian while earning his doctorate in Semitic studies at Harvard. Charles Forman was a founding member of the Unitarian Christian Fellowship. He served as pastor of The First Church of Plymouth, Massachusetts, (founded in 1630), until he went to Wheaton College, where he taught Arabic, Hebrew, Islam, Old Testament, and Religion and Literature.

He was affiliate minister of King's Chapel from 1977 until his death in 1998. In that position he led worship, preached, taught, counseled, and became a dearly beloved pastor.

The author of several prayers in our present prayer book, he is best remembered for the benediction that concludes several services in the prayer book and is inscribed on a plaque in the church's vestibule: "The Lord bless you and keep you. The Lord keep all those whom you love, whether here or in some other place. May God be your companion, and you be his friend, as you walk together through all the days of your life; and at the journey's end, may you find the welcome of God's love. It keeps us all. *Amen.*"

St. Francis of Assisi (c. 1181–1226)

The son of a wealthy merchant in Assisi, Francis worked in the family business by day and caroused at night until he joined the army. Combat and imprisonment sobered him, and upon his return home, he rebuilt and lived in a ruined chapel at Portiuncula, today a pilgrimage site. In this seclusion he read and pondered Christ's charge to his disciples in Matthew 10:5-10. Surrendering his patrimony, he devoted himself to prayer, personal poverty, and the poor wherever he met them.

Young men followed Francis into this dedicated life and in 1209 Pope Innocent III recognized this small band as a legitimate order, not one of

KEY FIGURES

monastic seclusion, but a company of brothers living in the world to serve the poor. Francis ruled this order for ten years but was eventually deposed by brothers who felt the order should acquire funds and property in order to be more effective. Almost blind, in pain, and disempowered, Francis died in the chapel at Portiuncula where he first read those prophetic verses from Matthew.

The prayer in the fifth litany, which begins "Lord, make us instruments of thy peace," is attributed to St. Francis.

Freeman, James (1759–1835)

Freeman grew up in Charlestown, the son of Lois Cobb Freeman and Constant Freeman, a sea captain and later a merchant in Charlestown and Quebec.

From 1767 through 1773 Freeman attended the Latin School, then located next to King's Chapel, and, subsequently, Harvard College. He excelled in languages and mathematics. While at Harvard his childhood home was destroyed when the British burned Charlestown just before the battle at Breed's (Bunker) Hill.

At age twenty-one Freeman went to visit his father in Quebec with the assurance that his Guarantee of Safety from the British in Boston would protect him. It did not, and he spent the next two years in Quebec, first on a prison ship and then on parole in the city. In 1782 he was released and returned to Massachusetts. His call to King's Chapel and his revision of the Anglican prayer book are described in The History of the Prayer Book in this book.

King's Chapel called Freeman to be a lay reader. In this role, he did not baptize, celebrate Holy Communion, or conduct weddings. From his arrival in 1782 until his ordination in 1787, King's Chapel continued without these services.

When the new American bishops, Samuel Seabury and Samuel Provoost, arrived in this country, Freeman sought ordination from them. Seabury refused to ordain him unless King's Chapel abandoned its new liturgy. Provoost neither refused nor consented, and Freeman returned to

KEY FIGURES

Boston still a layman. At this point the Proprietors of King's Chapel, impatient with delay, voted to ordain him themselves. They could have done this with blessing of the contiguous parish ministers, but that would have placed Freeman and the church squarely in the Puritan camp and precluded ordination by a bishop, which some parishioners still hoped for.

On November 16, 1787, Freeman was ordained without benefit of clergy either Episcopalian or Puritan. During his forty years at King's Chapel he never exchanged pulpits with another minister, not even with the Rev. Hosea Ballou, who founded the First Universalist Church just across School Street from King's Chapel.

Despite this inauspicious introduction, Freeman became an important citizen in Boston. He was a founder of the Massachusetts Historical Society and a member of the Boston Humane Society, the American Academy of Arts and Sciences, and the Massachusetts Peace Society. In 1792 he was elected to the city's first school committee. In 1813 he was chosen to preach at Boston's celebration of Napoleon's defeat in the Russian campaign and stunned the assembled two thousand with a passionate address comprised solely of verses selected from scripture and so arranged that they seemed to have been written specifically for that event.

In 1783 he married the widow Martha Curtis Clarke and adopted her nine-year old son Samuel. The family lived on Vine Street in Boston. Twenty years later when Samuel and his young wife had too many children and too little income, the Freemans bought Samuel's house in Newton and took his third child, James Freeman Clarke, into their home.

The couple raised this boy to adulthood. Freeman taught him Greek, Latin, history, science, and mathematics until he went to the Latin School from which Freeman himself had graduated. James Freeman Clarke went into the ministry, and in 1842 founded the Church of the Disciples on Beacon Street only one block up the hill from his step-grandfather's church.

Freeman died at age seventy-six and is buried in the Newton City Cemetery. His bust stands on the left side of the chancel.

KEY FIGURES

Greenwood, Francis William Pitt (1797–1843)

The only minister of King's Chapel who grew up in the church, Greenwood found an exemplar and mentor in his childhood pastor, James Freeman. As a child he memorized the catechism written by Joseph Priestley and printed in the 1785 prayer book.

After graduating from Harvard at age seventeen and reading theology with the Rev. Henry Ware Jr., Greenwood was called to the New South Church in Boston. His pastorate there was cut short at the age of twenty-two by a sudden "bleeding from the lungs." He spent the next two years convalescing in England. On his return to the United States he assisted his friend Jared Sparks at the Unitarian Church in Baltimore, where he met and married his wife. In 1824 Greenwood returned to Boston to become James Freeman's successor.

So great was anti-British sentiment after the Revolution that Bostonians, including King's Chapel parishioners, called the church building the Stone Chapel. This continued until the Rev. Greenwood suggested in a sermon that the church again be called King's Chapel, for, he said, "In King's Chapel, we worship the King of Kings."

Greenwood's ministry was halted at times by recurring attacks of tuberculosis, and in 1837 he spent a second convalescence in Cuba. Walking on the shores of that island and gathering shells gave him great pleasure. His portrait at the church's parish house shows a few seashells beside him. In spite of his debility and in addition to his work as pastor, preacher, and teacher at King's Chapel, Greenwood edited three editions of the prayer book, founded and taught Sunday School, and published three books of sermons—one a life of the apostles. He also compiled a hymnal used by several churches and wrote a short history of King's Chapel, which even now is a joy to read for its conciseness, clarity, and grace of style.

Greenwood preached his last sermon in 1842. He became an invalid at home where he died a year later. He was forty-six years old.

KEY FIGURES

Hermann of Wied (1477–1552)

Archbishop of Cologne by his late thirties, Hermann was for some time an enemy of Protestant leaders and churches in his diocese. But his desire to purify the Catholic liturgies made him more sympathetic to the Protestant cause, and he eventually sought the advice of Luther's colleagues, Martin Bucer and Philip Melanchthon, when he was considering his own proposals for liturgical reform. These were published in 1543 as *A Simple and Religious Consultation* and translated into English in 1548. Thomas Cranmer used several of his prayers in producing the second (1552) edition of the *Book of Common Prayer*. Hermann's sympathy with the Protestant cause occasioned his excommunication in 1546, and he died a Lutheran.

Three prayers from Hermann's *Consultation* appear in the King's Chapel prayer book: the long confirmation prayer on page 58, the general confession in the first order for Holy Communion on page 74, and the first confession in the second order for Holy Communion on page 86.

Hippolytus (c. 170–236)

A prolific theological writer, Hippolytus is best known as the author of *The Apostolic Tradition*, a description of the liturgy and other rituals of the Roman church in his time. He is also the author of *The Refutation of All Heresies*, a catalog and denunciation of at least ten Christian heresies, as well as the practices of diviners, magicians, astrologers, and two popes. His list of heresies reflects the wild variety of beliefs in the early church.

A theological maverick who refused to believe the holy Spirit was actually a person, Hippolytus was also a contentious critic of almost all his superiors, which may explain his eventual exile to the island of Sardinia, where he died. The phrase, "Lift up your hearts," and the response, "We lift them up onto the Lord," in Holy Communion come from this collection, as does the prayer, "We thank thee, O God," on page 38 in the King's Chapel prayer book.

KEY FIGURES

St. Jerome (342–420)

Upon his baptism as a young man, Jerome alternated between life as a monk and hermit on the one hand and travel on behalf of the church on the other. After serving for three years as secretary to Pope Damasus, Jerome went at age 44 to Bethlehem where he ruled a men's monastery and spent the rest of his years in study and writing.

His greatest work was translating into Latin the New Testament from Greek manuscripts and the Old Testament from Hebrew. He was a painstaking worker, making three separate translations of the psalms. His translation was called the Vulgate, so-called from the Latin word meaning "common" or "accessible." The Council of Trent made the Vulgate the official Latin Bible of the Roman Catholic Church, and it remained so until the Second Vatican Council. Jerome wrote commentaries on books of the Bible and translated works of church fathers who preceded him. He maintained an extensive correspondence with his theological contemporaries. Being a passionate Christian, he often attacked harshly those who differed with him. St. Augustine, for example, felt the sting of his pen more than once.

He is often portrayed with a lion sleeping at his feet. The lion in Saint Jerome rarely slept.

Julian of Norwich (c. 1342–after 1413)

At age 31, a young woman whose given name we do not know had a near-fatal illness during which she had sixteen visions of Christ on the cross. As a result, she became an anchoress, choosing to spend the rest of her life in a room attached to St. Julian's church in Norwich, England. She chose the saint's name as her own. During her confinement she wrote of her visions and their meaning in a book entitled *Revelations of Divine Love*, the first book written in English by a woman. Julian was not only an author, but also a spiritual guide and counselor. From her window looking onto Norwich's main street, she listened to and counseled people seeking her guidance. *Revelations of Divine Love* exists in many English translations. Her reconstructed cell in Norwich and the church itself, which was rebuilt after a World War II bombing, have become a pilgrimage site.

KEY FIGURES

Lindsey, Theophilus (1723–1808)

Lindsey was a liberal and a rational Anglican priest. Having chosen to be Unitarian, he resigned his priesthood in the village of Catterick and headed for London where he founded an independent church. On his way to London he visited an old friend, John Disney, who introduced him to Samuel Clarke's privately amended 1662 prayer book (see Clarke in this section.) Lindsey used this text for creating a radically altered Anglican service, which he used at his newly-founded church that still exists as the Essex Street Chapel.

A member of his congregation, William Hazzlitt, took a copy of this prayer book with him to America where he met James Freeman and offered the book as a model for Freeman's preparation of a new prayer book for King's Chapel.

Luther, Martin (1483–1546)

Trained in law and philosophy, Luther became an Augustinian monk and priest in his early thirties and taught for many years at the university in Wittenberg. His outrage at the corruption of the Roman church and the teaching of salvation by works, such as paying for indulgences, led him to oppose his bishop and the pope. In 1519 he denied the primacy of the pope and the infallibility of the general councils, the first being the council at Nicea in 325. This led to his excommunication in 1521. He became the preeminent reformer in the German states and the namesake of that country's national church.

Although an ecclesiastical radical, Luther was a liturgical conservative. The only initial change he made in the mass was to remove the long communion prayer in 1523. In its place he read an exhortation to receive not only the bread, but also the wine, formerly restricted to the clergy. In the words of Roland Bainton (*Here I Stand*, Abingdon Cokesbury, 1950, p. 339), "He restored the emphasis of the early Church upon the Lord's Supper as an act of thanksgiving to God and of fellowship through Christ with God and with each other."

KEY FIGURES

Luther soon realized that his largely unlettered congregation understood little of what was happening during the service, so in 1526 he translated the entire text of the mass into German. He had already translated the New Testament in 1522 and completed the Old Testament in 1534. German congregations began to hear the Gospel and Epistle in their own tongue and then a sermon, which interpreted the meaning of these lessons applied to their own lives. Scripture and sermon assumed the importance they had once had in the early church. The mass under Luther became not only an act of worship but a means of instruction as well.

Therefore, from its inception, Lutheran worship has been grounded in both scripture and in Holy Communion, called the Lord's Supper in that tradition. Luther's *German Mass* and Thomas Cranmer's *Book of Common Prayer* created the two great Protestant prayer book traditions.

By contrast, the Presbyterian, Reform, Congregational, Anabaptist, Methodist, and evangelical and charismatic churches follow a tradition of "free" worship, based on scripture, preaching, prayer, and hymnody, but with widely different liturgical styles.

Martineau, James (1805–1900)

After serving Unitarian churches in Dublin and Liverpool, Martineau then taught philosophy at the Unitarian seminary in Manchester and later became its dean. An ardent theist, he argued against the scientific materialism of Darwin's disciples. His long walks in the hills and mountains of England may also have witnessed to his faith in God's goodness. He wrote some beautiful prayers, including one that begins, "Eternal God, who committest to us the swift and solemn trust of life, since we know not what a day may bring forth, but only that the hour for serving thee is always present, may we wake to the instant claims of thy holy will, not waiting for tomorrow, but yielding today." This prayer may be found on page 179 of the prayer book.

KEY FIGURES

Neale, John Mason (1818–1866)

Ordained in the Church of England at age 24, Neale was denied advancement in that church because of his High Church tendencies, and for the last twenty years of his life lived on twenty-eight pounds a year as warden of a home for indigent elderly men. This position left him time to pursue his consuming interest in hymnody and liturgy.

He translated many ancient Greek and Latin hymns into English and wrote a five-volume history of the Eastern church and a four-volume commentary on the psalms. He wrote many hymns, including "Good King Wenceslas," "Come, ye faithful, raise the strain," and "All glory, laud, and honor." He copyrighted none of them, explaining he was casting his two mites into the Lord's treasury.

In 1854 he founded a teaching and nursing order, the Sisters of St. Margaret, which now has houses in Dedham Massachusetts, and Haiti. Never blessed with good health, Neale died at the age of 48.

Newman, Henry Cardinal (1801–1890)

A popular preacher at Oxford University, Newman was a leader in the Oxford Movement, which aimed to renew Anglican worship through a rich ceremonial, and celebrated communion every week instead of monthly or quarterly, as most Church of England churches did at the time. After six disappointing years as a priest in the Church of England, Newman astounded his colleagues and the public by converting to Catholicism.

Although a new convert, Newman vigorously opposed the expansion of power that Pope Pius IX sought at the First Vatican Council. In this effort John Lord Acton, his fellow countryman and ally, wrote the aphorism often quoted in political campaigns by whatever party is not in power: "Power corrupts, and absolute power corrupts absolutely."

Newman either wrote or translated from Latin the prayer, "O Lord, support us all the day long," found at the end of the burial service.

KEY FIGURES

Origen (185–c. 254)

A theologian and biblical scholar in the city of Alexandria, Origen taught the doctrine of *apocatastasis*, which he learned from his teacher Clement. This doctrine holds that at the end of time, everyone, including the demons and the devil himself, will be restored to God. Gregory of Nyssa (330–395) and Cyril of Alexandria (d. 444) also taught this doctrine, which was attacked by Augustine and others, and declared heretical by the Council of Constantinople in 543. Origen, an extreme ascetic, survived torture during the persecution of Decius in 250, but died a few years later.

St. Paul (died c. 67)

Born Saul, a Roman citizen, Paul grew up in Tarsus, a city in Asia Minor, now Turkey. As a young man and zealous Jew, he hunted and persecuted Christians and turned them over to civil authorities, as described in Acts 8:1, 9:1-2 and by himself in I Corinthians 15:9 and Galatians 1:13-14. Later in life he experienced a powerful conversion experience to Christianity. (See Acts 9:3-9, II Corinthians 12:2-4) As Paul, he preached, founded, and visited new churches in Athens, Colossae, Corinth, Galatia, Philippi, Thessalonica, Ephesus, and Rome, where he may have died a martyr during Nero's persecution.

He tells us he was "rude in speech" (II Corinthians 10:10), and afflicted by an unspecified "thorn in the flesh." (II Corinthians 12: 7-10) He was passionate in his care for his young churches and willing to suffer much for them. (II Corinthians 11: 23-29) His early training in Jewish theology and scripture served him well in interpreting Christian faith and practice, not only to the new Christians in his time, but in our time as well.

Paul was one of the first missionaries, along with Peter, Barnabas, Timothy, Titus, Apollos, Sosthenes, and others, but only his letters to the seven churches that he founded and to his three colleagues, Titus, Timothy, and Philemon, have survived. These letters are a primer in Christian theology and ethics.

KEY FIGURES

From these letters come two benedictions often heard at the end of Christian worship, namely: "The grace of our Lord Jesus Christ, the love of God and the fellowship of the holy Spirit be with you all evermore." (II Corinthians 13:14) The other is: "The peace of God which passeth all understanding keep your hearts and minds through Jesus Christ our Lord." (Philippians 4:7) This is usually expanded as found at the end of the Second Order of Communion.

From his second letter to the (1 Corinthians 11: 23b-25), written about 55 CE, come the Words of Institution in Holy Communion: "The Lord Jesus the same night that he was betrayed took bread: and when he had given thanks, he broke it, and said, 'Take eat: this is my body, which is broken for you. This do in remembrance of me.' After the same manner also he took the cup, when he had supped, saying, 'This cup is the new testament in my blood. This do as oft as ye drink it, in remembrance of me.'"

Perkins, Palfrey (1883–1976)

The minister of King's Chapel from 1933 to 1953, the Rev. Perkins never altered the text of the services, but he read them Sunday after Sunday as though reading them for the first time. In so doing, he imparted life and intelligence to these ancient words. The prayer book lives today due, in part, to him.

He was active in the civic life of Boston, serving on the boards of the Boston Symphony, the Boston Public Library, Wellesley College, and the Boston Urban League.

Priestley, Joseph (1733–1804)

Although known for his scientific work, specifically his discovery of oxygen, Priestley was also a preacher. He founded the Unitarian Society in England in 1791, but when he defended the French Revolution in 1794, he aroused such mob hostility that he left the country for the United States. He served a small Unitarian church in Northumberland, Pennsylvania, for the last ten years of his life. Priestley wrote a lovely catechism for children, which was published in the first few editions of the King's Chapel prayer book.

KEY FIGURES

Priscillian (died c. 385)

A Spanish layman who later became bishop of Avila, Priscillian gained many followers of his unusual and perhaps heretical version of Christianity. Charged with heresy and practicing magic, he was convicted by an ecclesiastical court in Bordeaux and executed in 385. This was the first time that the Christian church punished a heretic with death. The heresy itself continued well into the sixth century.

Quinones, Francisco (died 1540)

Made a cardinal in 1528, Quinones devoted himself to the reformation of the mass. His new breviary abolished the celebrations of lesser saints and required recitation of the whole Psalter in the course of a week as well as the reading of the entire Bible in the course of a year. Cranmer borrowed from this breviary in compiling the *Book of Common Prayer*. Quinones' breviary was proscribed by the pope in 1558.

Scovel, Carl (1932–)

Born and raised in China where his parents were medical missionaries, he served The First Parish of Sudbury for ten years before coming to King's Chapel in 1967. He edited *The Unitarian Christian* for six years and preached in more than a hundred Unitarian Universalist churches, interpreting Christian faith to non-Christian congregations. For twenty-two years on Sunday mornings he spoke for five minutes on WCRB radio. Some of these talks were later published in a collection entitled *Never Far From Home*. He chaired the committee that produced the ninth edition of the prayer book in 1986. After retiring in 1999, he has concentrated on spiritual direction and teaching.

Servetus, Michael (1511–1553)

Born in Spain and trained in his youth for a career in the Spanish court, he privately studied the New Testament. Since he could find there no explicit teaching of the Trinity, he deemed that doctrine invalid, and in 1531 published *On the Errors of the Trinity*. In this book he argued

KEY FIGURES

that Jesus was not the Eternal Son of God, but the Son of the Eternal God.

So great was the wrath of both Protestant and Catholic readers that Servetus fled to Paris where he studied medicine and for twelve years practiced in Lyons. But he continued his theological studies and in 1553 published *The Restitution of Christianity*. In this book he not only continued his attack on the Trinity, but also challenged the divinity of Jesus and the practice of infant baptism.

He was caught by the Spanish Inquisition but escaped from prison and fled to Geneva where he was again imprisoned. John Calvin, the religious leader of that city, pressed the town council to execute him, and at length they did. He was burned at the stake in Geneva on October 27, 1553. He was heard to cry from the flames "Jesus, Son of the Eternal God, have mercy on me." His last words were thus a protest and an affirmation of his faith.

We might never know of Servetus had not Sebastian Castellio, hearing of his death, written *Concerning Heretics*. In that book Castellio denounced the decision to burn Servetus and pleaded the cause of religious liberty. Thanks to him and other free spirits Servetus is now a hero in Unitarian Universalist churches.

Socinus, Faustus (1539–1604)

A native of Siena in northern Italy, then a hotbed of radical Catholic thinkers, Socinus, at age 23, published a commentary on the Gospel of John in which he denied the divinity of Christ. After studying at Basel he went to Transylvania hoping to find a welcome among the Unitarians, then led by their founder, Francis David. When a new king came to power and imprisoned David, Socinus fled to Cracow, Poland. There his philosophy took root among the Polish Brethren in the Minor Reformed Church of that country. From Poland, Socinianism spread to the Netherlands and eventually to England and the United States, where it took the form of Unitarianism.

KEY FIGURES

Stoddard, Solomon (1643–1729)

For fifty-five years the pastor of the church in Northampton, Massachusetts, Stoddard combined evangelical sermons with a generous heart. Although his Boston in-laws, the Reverends Cotton and Increase Mather, offered communion only to those who could claim and prove a powerful experience of conversion, Stoddard admitted to communion any church member not guilty of scandalous behavior. For him, communion was not a reward for the spiritual elite but a means of converting ordinary Christians to deeper faith. Four years before his death, he chose his grandson, a recent graduate of Yale, to be his assistant and eventual successor. That grandson was Jonathan Edwards.

Stokes, Harry (1930–1993)

A lover of books and learning, Harry Stokes opened a bookstore at Harvard Divinity School while a student there. Upon graduation in 1959 and after his experience as a seminarian in three Unitarian churches, he decided that parish ministry was not for him. He taught at private and public schools in Boston and Cambridge until his retirement.

At King's Chapel he was for eight years the church school director and lay reader, the first to serve in the latter capacity since James Freeman. He amassed a large scholarly library and became the authoritative voice on matters liturgical and theological for the 1986 prayer book committee. An invaluable member, he wrote at least a dozen prayers and propers for the present edition.

KEY FIGURES

Tertullian, Quintus Septimius (c. 160–c. 220)

Educated as a pagan, Tertullian in his mid-thirties became a Christian and the church's most prolific and passionate defender. His first work, *The Apology*, aimed to show Roman prefects how ridiculous were the accusations brought against Christians. Tertullian argued that Christians were good citizens and monotheists, who could not give divine honors to any emperor. He described the life of Christian communities and argued that persecution would only increase their numbers, since "the blood of the martyrs is the seed of the church."

In his second work, *Prescriptions Against Heretics*, Tertullian laid out the beliefs of the church by which unorthodox views were deemed heretical. He wrote specific treatises against two Gnostic leaders, Marcion and Praxeas, and two extended essays on baptism and penance. The first church father to write in Latin, not Greek, he also was the first to use the word "trinity" in describing the three persons of the Godhead.

King's Chapel, New England's first Anglican Church,
was established in 1686 and occupied this
wooden building at the foot of Beacon Hill in 1689.

In 1754 the parishioners moved into the present sanctuary,
which was designed by Peter Harrison and built with granite
from the Quincy quarries. It became known as the Stone Chapel
after the Revolutionary War because of strong anti-Royalist
sentiment. The Reverend Greenwood led the movement to
return to the church's original name, explaining that
"in King's Chapel we worship the King of Kings."

GLOSSARY

Abbey – The house of a monastic order. For those called to this life, men or women, it is their home, school, church, work place, infirmary, and final resting place.

Agnus Dei – Literally, "Lamb of God," this brief prayer, based on John 1:29, is part of most Western celebrations of the Eucharist. The phrase, "Lamb of God who takes away the sins of the world" is said or chanted three times. The people respond to the first two recitations: "Lord, have mercy upon us," and to the last, "Grant us thy peace."

Alleluia – Also "Hallelujah." From the Hebrew imperative, "Praise ye Yah (*Yahweh*)," this phrase appears mostly in the psalms, especially Psalms 111–117, known as "the Hallel psalms." Elsewhere in the Bible the word "Hallelujah" appears only in the apocryphal book of Tobit 13:18 and in Revelation 19:1, 3, 4, and 6 where the angels in heaven sing this chant. Many scholars believe that the heavenly worship reported in the book of Revelation reflects the worship services of the first Christians.

Amen – A Hebrew term of strong assent, meaning "truly, definitely." See Deuteronomy 27:15-26 for examples. It became the congregation's response to the leader's prayers (Romans 15:30, I Corinthians 14:16, *Didache* 10:6), the ending to a doxology (Romans 1:25), or a blessing (Galatians 6:18). Jesus often began a serious teaching by saying "Amen, amen," usually translated "Truly, truly," or "Verily, verily."

The first Christians saw Jesus himself as the Amen to God's will. St. Paul speaks of "Christ in whom all God's promises find their Amen." (Romans 15:8) Revelation 3:14 says, "Here is the message of Amen, the true and faithful witness."

Anamnesis – This word is usually translated "remember," as in Jesus's words at the Last Supper, "take this in remembrance of me." However, Kittell's Greek dictionary says, "In the New Testament 'to remember' is not just a mental act." *Anamnesis* is a memory that becomes alive and real

GLOSSARY

in present action. Therefore, when we celebrate Holy Communion, we are not just thinking of Jesus's last supper with his disciples. We relive that meal with each other, trusting that Christ is among us as we do so.

Anathema – In the New Testament this was either a curse (I Corinthians 12:3, 16:22) or a solemn oath (Acts 23:12,21). In 306 CE the Council of Elvira decreed temporary or lifetime banishment from the church for heresy or misbehavior, calling this act anathematization. While excommunication meant exclusion from all Christian worship, the ban of anathema excluded one from any kind of association with the Christian community.

Angel – The English word "angel" is the equivalent of the Hebrew word *malachi*, which means "a messenger." An angel therefore is a messenger from God, who often appears as a human being, as in the three visitors who tell Abraham and Sarah that she shall bear a son (Genesis 18:1-14) or the mysterious being who wrestles with Jacob in the darkness. (Genesis 32: 24-30)

Winged angels are rare in the Bible. In Genesis we read of only two— the cherub (plural, cherubim) who guards the entrance to Eden after God expels Adam and Eve and the flaming creature called a seraph (plural, seraphim) in Isaiah 6:6. In the temple Isaiah sees the seraphim covering themselves with their six wings and hears them singing "Holy, holy, holy."

When the Jewish scriptures were translated into Greek, the word *malachi* became *angelos*, which later became the Latin *angelus*. All these words mean "messenger." At some point in history artists began to paint angels with wings, and that image is now stuck in our minds. But God's messengers can appear in any guise.

Anglican – This term usually refers to the established Church of England and all churches around the world in communion with the Church of England. Break-away Episcopal churches in the U.S. have adopted this title in order to distinguish themselves from the American Protestant Episcopal Church. In this book we use "Anglican" to refer to the liturgies and traditions inherited from the Church of England.

GLOSSARY

Antiphon – A short text said or sung by the choir or congregation in response to a longer text said or sung by a cantor or a member of the clergy. The antiphon in Psalm 136 is "for his mercy endureth forever." The antiphon in the third litany in the prayer book is "Good Lord, deliver us."

Apocalypse – The Greek word means a "revelation" or "unveiling." Although it often suggests a disastrous ending to a civilization or history, it is also a literary term. An apocalyptic writer is one who describes a past event as if it were happening in the present or future.

For example, the author of the book of Daniel wrote a story about heroic Jews who witnessed to their faith during the Babylonian captivity. But he did so four hundred years after the captivity, when Israel had been invaded by the Syrian army. These armies abused the people and defiled the temple by keeping pigs there. Jews who read the book of Daniel knew that this story, set in the past, was a call to arms against their oppressors.

Apocrypha – This word, meaning "that which is hidden away," refers to books not accepted into the canon of authorized scripture. Apocryphal books are those whose legitimacy as scripture is debated. Jewish scholars in Jerusalem were disinclined to accept them as scripture, while those in Babylon included them.

The Jewish Apocrypha appeared between 300 and 400 BCE. These are books of teachings, legends, history, and pseudo-history. All but one of these books were included in the definitive Greek translation of the Jewish scriptures, the Septuagint.

The Christian church accepted most of the Jewish Apocrypha into its canon. St. Jerome did so in his translation of the Christian scriptures from Greek into Latin in the year 400. This translation was called the Vulgate because Jerome wrote in the common or "vulgar" Latin that the people spoke, not in the classical Latin in which scholars wrote. It was the official Bible of the Christian church for more than a thousand years.

Most Protestant reformers rejected the Jewish Apocrypha and did not publish these books in their translations of the Vulgate into French and

GLOSSARY

German. The King James Bible included the Jewish Apocrypha in a special section, and the 1549 *Book of Common Prayer* included several readings from it. Recent Protestant translations of the Bible have included as many as twenty books from the Jewish Apocrypha, usually printed in a separate section.

There is also a Christian Apocrypha, consisting of Gospels, letters, legends, teachings, and other writings. Professor Willis Barnstone of Yale (1927–) has translated and collected forty of these books in *The Other Bible* and prefaced each with a brief commentary.

Apostle – The Greek word *apostello* means "to send out." An *apostolos* is "one who is sent." In Matthew 10:5-23 Jesus sends out his disciples to preach, heal, and exorcise evil spirits. Thereafter they are called apostles. In the early church an apostle was one commissioned with a ministry, usually to preach.

The Apostolic Tradition (c. 350 CE) – A collection of early Christian rules, prayers, and other liturgical materials written and/or compiled by Hippolytus, a brilliant and irascible theologian in Rome, whose criticisms of four successive popes may have caused his eventual exile to Sardinia.

The Apostolic Tradition is an invaluable guide to the faith and worship of the early church. From this collection comes the prayer, "We thank Thee, O God," at the beginning of Evensong and the versicles beginning with "Lift up your hearts" in Holy Communion.

Arian – A follower of the teachings of Arius. See the entry in Key Figures.

Authorized Version – This is the English name of what we in the United States call the King James Bible. This translation was made by six committees of scholars who met for more than three years at Oxford and Cambridge universities and Westminster Abbey. They translated from the Greek, Latin, and Hebrew texts available at that time. The final version was published in 1611 with the blessing of King James I. See

GLOSSARY

God's Secretaries, by Adam Nicolson, published in 2001, for an interesting account of its creation.

Baptizand – One who is about to be or has just been baptized.

BCE – This abbreviation means "Before the Common Era." CE refers to the "Common Era." These abbreviations are now preferred by style guides for religious texts. They are used instead of BC for "Before Christ" or AD, for "Anno Domini," meaning "in the year of the Lord." That traditional count of the years was established in the sixth-century by a Christian monk, Dionysius Exiguus, who made the beginning of Jesus' life the reference date.

The word "common" is seen as more inclusive of other religions than the traditional terms. But the years are still measured in terms of Christ's birth.

Benediction – Literally "a good word," a benediction is the pronouncement of God's blessing upon a congregation, usually at the end of a service. Recently and most unfortunately, a benediction has become a synopsis of the sermon or an exhortation to do good.

Bible – The word comes from the plural, *biblion*, of the Greek *biblos*, which originally meant "made from papyrus bark." Later, the same word applied to bibles written or printed on parchment, vellum, or paper. The Old Testament contains thirty-nine books, comprising more than three-fourths of the Bible. The New Testament has twenty-seven books. In addition to these, the Authorized Version includes most of the Old Testament Apocrypha. The current Roman Catholic Bible includes several books from this Apocrypha. (See Apocrypha in this Glossary.)

Although the Bible has sixty-six books, it is more than a collection. Many authors were deeply immersed in the text and faith of earlier books. The themes and metaphors in the Bible weave in and out of the whole book, creating a fabric of both obvious and subtle cross-references. Every

GLOSSARY

passage in the Bible should be read in the context of the entire narrative, a story that begins in a garden, moves to the city and ends in heaven. See also Translations in this section.

Breviary – A liturgical book containing the psalms, chants, hymns, prayers, and lessons to be read or sung at the daily services, called "offices," which are held in monasteries, abbeys, or cathedrals.

Canon – A *kanon* in Greek was a measuring rod or a carpenter's rule. It came to mean a code of laws or a standard of judgment. "Canon" can mean three different things in church usage: those books authorized as scripture, the Eucharistic prayers that follow the *Sanctus* in the mass, or clergy serving in a cathedral.

Canticle – From the Latin *canticulum*, the diminutive of *cantus*, meaning "song," this word describes a non-psalm text found in scripture and arranged to be sung in a liturgy.

Cantor – The leader of congregational singing in a liturgy.

Carolingian – During his reign from 768 to 814, Charlemagne, through his advisers, Alcuin and Theodolf of Orleans, instituted a huge educational and liturgical reform of the services and ministries of the clergy in all abbeys and churches in France. This revival, named Carolingian for Charlemagne, continued long after his death and made France a major center of learning in the Middle Ages.

Catechumen – This word from the Greek word, *katacheo*, meaning "to instruct," describes "those who are being instructed," namely, candidates for baptism who were or are learning the faith and doctrines of the church.

    Until recently catechumens were allowed to attend only the first part of the liturgy, when they learned the faith of the church from the prayers, lessons, and sermon. After the sermon, catechumens were dismissed from the service. On the eve of Epiphany, Easter, or Pentecost, they were baptized and then received their first communion.

Cathari – A medieval sect that appeared in Germany, northern Italy, and southern France in the late 1100s. The name derives from the Greek word *catharos* meaning "the pure." In their reaction against the church's corruption and the disastrous Second Crusade, the Cathari tried to live pure lives that would free them from the evil power that ruled this world.

Its most zealous members avoided marriage, oaths, war, and wealth, and lived on a lacto-vegetarian diet. More lax members were allowed to compromise on these issues. Cathari worship was simple, and placed the Gospel of John above all scriptures. The Cathari aroused so violent a response from the Catholic church that within a century it was completely destroyed by persecutions. John Milton, remembering their slaughter, wrote a poem that begins "Avenge, O Lord, Thy slaughter'd saints whose bones lie scatter'd on the Alpine mountains cold . . ."

CE – See BCE.

Ceremonial – This word has two meanings. It may refer to such liturgical actions as bowing, kneeling, crossing oneself, censing the altar and icons, elevating the host and chalice, and processing the Bible. It may also refer to the general tradition of liturgical observance in a given church, cathedral, abbey or household of faith, e.g., "The ceremonial in a cathedral is often ornate."

Ceremony – A specific religious service or observance, usually conducted in a formal manner.

Cherubim – see Angel.

Christ – The Greek *christos*, comes from the verb, *crio*, meaning "to smear, rub, or anoint." It therefore means "one who is anointed." In Israel

GLOSSARY

candidates for kingship or the priesthood assumed such positions by being anointed by a prophet or later a priest. When the Jewish people began to look forward to a future deliverer, they called him "the anointed one, in Hebrew *Messias* or in English, "the Messiah."

The first Christians saw Jesus as the Messiah, anointed to deliver them, not from Roman rule but from bondage to sin. Christians saw Jesus Christ as the one who embodied the realm of God's righteousness. Hence, Tertullian's adage, "Jesus Christ is the kingdom of God in person."

Church fathers – This term describes the theologians of the early church, usually bishops, who discussed, debated, and defined the basic articles of Christian faith. They include St. Augustine (354–430), Cyprian (c. 200–258), John Chrysostom (347–407), John of Damascus (675–749), Tertullian (c. 155–240), the Cappadocian fathers, and many lesser-known figures during those centuries.

Churching of Women – A service of blessing and thanksgiving for women after childbirth.

Clerk – Also called the parish clerk, this position in Anglican churches was usually held by a lay person who cared for the church premises, read the Epistle lesson at services, and led the congregation's responses.

Collect – A collect is a short prayer with all or most of five elements as seen in the Collect for Peace: a title by which we address God, "O God;" an attribution by which we understand God, "unto whom all hearts are open, all desires known and from whom no secrets are hid;" a petition, "cleanse the thoughts of our hearts by the inspiration of thy holy Spirit;" a desired result of that petition, "that we may perfectly love thee and worthily magnify thy holy name;" and a conclusion, "through Jesus Christ our Lord, Amen."

GLOSSARY

Compline – The eighth and last of the daily offices, said or sung before sleep in abbeys and monasteries. An office consists of psalms, a chant, a canticle, and prayers. Roman Catholic monasteries and abbeys often conclude this office with a hymn to the Virgin Mary.

Confession – The word means "to acknowledge, confide, or witness." Thus, one declares one's faith by a confession. One also confesses one's sins to God in the presence of a priest.

Confessor – This term can describe the one to whom one makes a confession. It also may describe someone who has suffered for his or her faith, but did not die as a martyr.

Convent – This word refers either to the buildings or the community of a religious order. Although the word originally referred to either a male or female order, it now usually means an order of nuns.

Covenant – See the section on Covenants, Confessions, and Creeds.

Decalogue – From the Greek for ten words, or sayings, this means the Ten Commandments. These commandments are found in Exodus 20:1-17 and Deuteronomy 5:6-21. See the commentary in the last litany described in the Components of Worship section.

Didache – Pronounced "deedakay," this second-century manual of morals and practice, discovered in 1873, is the earliest known Christian liturgical text. In its first chapters it describes the Way of Life and the Way of Death. It then provides instruction on baptism, fasting, and prayer, as well as guidelines for bishops and deacons and directions for celebrating the Eucharist. The *Didache* recommends that Christians say the Lord's Prayer as found in Matthew 6:9-13 three times daily.

There follow two examples of the Eucharistic prayers in this collection. "With regard to the Eucharist this is the way you should give

GLOSSARY

thanks. First, for the chalice. 'We give you thanks, Father, for the holy vine of your servant David, which you made known through your servant Jesus. Glory to you throughout the ages.' And 'for the broken bread. We give you thanks, Father, for the life and knowledge which you sent us through your servant Jesus. Glory to you throughout the ages.' "

Doxology – This Greek word means "a word, or act, of adoration," denoting a brief act of praise. The word, "Alleluia," may be the shortest doxology. Both testaments abound with doxologies, including those that conclude the five sections of the Psalms, 1-41, 42-72, 73-89, 90-106 and 107-150. Not all New Testament doxologies are directed to God through Christ, for example, Revelation 5:12.

Given James Freeman's decision to include only "doxologies from the pure word of God," it is not surprising that he dropped the Gloria Patri from the 1785 prayer book, since it cannot be found in scripture.

In its place Freeman inserted a verse from I Timothy 1:17: "To the King of ages, immortal, invisible, the only God, be honor and glory forever and ever. Amen." At some point "only" was altered to "only wise," meaning "in the only way."

Freeman found this doxology in a prayer book the Rev. Theophilus Lindsey prepared for his chapel at Essex Street in London. Lindsey found it in a 1662 prayer book that the Rev. Samuel Clarke, rector of St. James's Church, Piccadilly, privately amended in 1727.

Clarke himself may have found this doxology in *A Collection of Private Devotions* compiled in 1627 by the Rev. John Cosin, at one time bishop of Durham and a strict high churchman.

Easter – The English and Germanic name for the day of resurrection. According to the English church historian, St. Bede (673–735), the name comes from an Anglo-Saxon goddess, *Eostre*, whose annual rites were held at the spring equinox. The name may also come from the Old English *eastre*, meaning east, referring to an ancient goddess of the dawn. In either case or any, this seems to be an example of Christians taking over a pagan

GLOSSARY

practice. Only English speaking and Germanic cultures use this name. For the others, see *Pascha*.

Eastern – The Christian churches and liturgical traditions of Eastern Europe and the Near East. Governed by the bishops within a given country, these Eastern or Orthodox churches are found in Greece, Russia, Romania, Hungary, Turkey, Syria, and Lebanon. Eastern churches evolved slowly over the last two thousand years, having had neither a reformation nor a counter-reformation. They broke with the Western church, then governed by the pope, in 1054. The churches in these nations are self-governing but owe at least some allegiance to the patriarch in either Moscow or Istanbul, a situation that often becomes a serious political issue.

Elements – Along with other meanings, this word refers to the bread and wine administered in Holy Communion.

Encomia – The plural of encomium, meaning an act of formal praise or a tribute.

Epiphany – From a Greek word meaning "manifestation" or "disclosing," this feast day on January 6 began among the Eastern churches as a celebration of Christ's birth and baptism. Eventually the Western churches chose December 25, the Roman festival of the unconquered sun, *sol invictus*, as the day of Christ's birth. So, in the West, Epiphany became the celebration of Christ's manifestation to the non-Jewish peoples, who were called Gentiles, from the Latin *gens, gentis* meaning "nations or races." The magi from the East represented these peoples. Epiphany also celebrates Christ's miracle at the wedding feast in Cana. A medieval hymn combines Christ's baptism, the wedding feast, and the magi in a single verse:

> Today the church is joined with her spouse
> Because Christ has been washed of his guilt;
> The kings hasten with gifts to the wedding feast,
> And the guests rejoice because water has been turned into wine.

GLOSSARY

Eucharist – The Greek word means "the thanksgiving." Called Holy Communion in the Anglican communion, the liturgy in Orthodox churches, the mass in Catholic churches, and the Lord's Supper in Protestant and Evangelical churches, this is the unique and defining act of worship in Christian churches. The earliest record of this service is found in I Corinthians 11:23-26. The three synoptic Gospels (Matthew 26:26-29, Mark 14:22-25, and Luke 22:14-20) record the institution of the Eucharist in Christ's last supper with his disciples.

Gelasian Sacramentary – Attributed to Pope Gelasius, who served from 492 to 496, this collection of prayers and the first complete text of the mass were likely the work of several priests in Rome. This sacramentary was the authoritative source for Eucharistic celebrations until the 1200s. Many of its prayers appeared in the *Book of Common Prayer* and sixteen prayers in the present King's Chapel prayer book come from this source.

Gloria in Excelsis – Also called the Greater Doxology or the Angelic Hymn. Based on the angels' song in Luke 2:14, it has been sung in the Eastern church since the fourth century. The King's Chapel prayer book included it in Holy Communion but dropped two ancient prayers, the *Kyrie Eleison* (Lord, have mercy) and the *Agnus Dei* (Lamb of God). Presently this chant closes the first order of Holy Communion at King's Chapel and opens the second order. Its authorship and age are unknown.

Gloria Patri – Also called the Lesser Doxology, this short hymn of praise concluded the recitation of psalms as early as the fourth century. The full text is "Glory be to the Father and to the Son and to the holy Spirit; As it was in the beginning is now and ever shall be, world without end, Amen."

Gnosticism – See the section on Creeds under Components of Worship in the text.

GLOSSARY

Gospels – The Gospels are the first four books of the New Testament: Matthew, Mark, Luke, and John. The word is derived from the Old English godspel meaning "good news." It is a translation of the Greek *evangelion*, which means the proclamation of good news. An *evangelion* might be a military victory or the birth or enthronement of an emperor. St. Paul, writing to the young churches in the first half of the first century, used this word to describe the good news of Jesus, God's Word, come to a suffering world.

Writing twenty years later, the author of Mark opens his book with these words: "The beginning of the Gospel of Jesus Christ." The four books witnessing to Jesus were not themselves called Gospels until about 150 CE. By then they were recognized as the authoritative witness to the One who was and is the center of all Christian faith.

These four Gospels were carefully edited collections of Jesus' followers' memories of his teachings, arguments, healings, friendships, enemies, conversations, death, and his return. These memories were written down, first as separate fragments that were later collected into a narrative. In making these collections the Gospel writers created a unique literary form. For the Gospels are not biography, philosophy, mythology, or ethical manuals. They are the written witness to the encounter between a real man who was also God's Word and those who had been so changed by knowing him that they could never be the same again. No literary form like this had ever appeared before.

These four collections were attributed to and named for certain exemplary apostles. Mark was the earliest Gospel, usually dated shortly after 70 CE. Matthew and Luke followed Mark's narrative, but also drew from a common collection of teachings called Q (from the German *Quelle* meaning "source.") Half of Luke and a quarter of Matthew come from their own unique sources.

Compared to John, the first three Gospels are so similar that they are called the Synoptic Gospels from the Greek *syn* (together) and *optic* (seeing). John is a carefully constructed work written about 100 CE for the growing number of non-Jewish Christians. It is rich in teachings, usually

GLOSSARY

connected with a miracle. Often John's Gospel takes a different tack from the Synoptic Gospels. For example, in place of the blessing of the bread and wine at the Last Supper, John tells how Jesus washed the feet of his disciples.

But all four books are Gospels. They tell the good news of Jesus. We said that Mark opens his book with the words, "The beginning of the good news of Jesus Christ." He does not, however, conclude his book with "The end of the Gospel of Jesus Christ." The reason for this must be obvious.

Gregorian Sacramentary – This collection of prayers and services, compiled during the reign of Pope Gregory I (540–604), was for six hundred years the definitive liturgical text for the Christian church in the West and became an important source for Thomas Cranmer's revision of the English liturgy.

Hail Mary – This short prayer is based on the angel Gabriel's greeting to Mary in Luke 1:28. It is said in Catholic and Anglo-Catholic liturgies and as a private devotion by members of those churches. Its use as a popular devotion began in the twelfth century; in its present form it was blessed by the pope in 1658.

High Church – This term describes a church or tradition with an elaborate ceremonial, often a reconstruction of an earlier form of worship. Such practice is often accompanied with a clearly articulated doctrine of the church and sacraments.

Holy – The Hebrew word translated as "holy" is *kadosh*, and may come from a verb meaning to cut or divide. Hence, *kadosh* or holy means that which is set apart from common, ordinary, daily use. A particular food, utensil, place, practice, ritual, person, people, action, or word may be holy, thus consecrated to the worship or service of God.

GLOSSARY

Host – The bread used in the Eucharist once it is consecrated and thus becomes, literally or figuratively, the body of Christ. The term comes from the Latin *hostia* meaning "a sacrificial victim."

Intercessions – Prayers offered on behalf of another person, people, effort, or institution. In Morning Prayer we pray through a series of collects for all nations, those in authority, clergy, congregations and all sorts and conditions of humanity. In the First Order of Holy Communion we pray for the same through a single extended prayer and in the Second Order the same through a set of versicles and responses.

Jesus – Jesus is the English rendering of *iesous*, which is Greek for the Hebrew name *Yehoshuah*, meaning, "*Yahweh* will save, or saves, or is salvation." It was a common name in the first century.

Jesus Prayer – Also known as the prayer of the heart, this prayer, "Lord Jesus Christ, have mercy on me," has been said by Orthodox Christians since at least 600 CE, the date of its earliest text. It is based on Luke 18:10-14, where the publican says the following prayer, "Lord, have mercy on me, a sinner." St. Gregory Palamas defended its frequent repetition as a means of coming closer to God. *The Diary of a Pilgrim*, written by a simple, literate peasant in the mid-nineteenth century, is a charming account of the author's wanderings across the face of Russia as he learns to make this prayer the heart of his life.

King James Version – See Authorized Version

Kyrie Eleison – This phrase, meaning "Lord, have mercy," appeared in the Syrian church in the fourth century and made its way into the liturgies of the Eastern and Western churches. In the Catholic, Anglican, Lutheran, and Episcopalian liturgies it is part of a nine-fold repetition, alternating between the phrases "Christ, have mercy" and "Lord have mercy." In the Eastern liturgy this phrase is the congregation's usual response to the prayers in several litanies.

GLOSSARY

Lauds – This early morning office is read or sung in abbeys and cathedrals. The word is derived from the Latin, *laudate*, the imperative of the verb, "praise." It is found in Psalms 148 through 150, which are sung at lauds. Thomas Cranmer combined parts of matins, lauds, and prime to create Morning Prayer for the 1549 *Book of Common Prayer*.

Lectio divina – Literally, "holy reading," this term describes the practice of contemplative reading of the Bible, the writings of the church fathers, and other devotional books. Such reading is quiet, slow, solitary, reflective, and prayerful. Its aim is to let the text inhabit the reader, allowing the soul of the text to speak to the soul of the reader.

Leonine Sacramentary – This collection of prayers and services, authorized by Pope Leo I (c. 440–461), was in use by the church for at least eight hundred years. The earliest copy of it, made in the seventh century, still exists.

Litany – A litany is a form of prayer in which the priest, deacon, or minister bids the congregation to pray for a series of specific intentions, the people responding with such phrases as "Lord, have mercy," "Lord, hear our prayer," or "Grant this, O Lord."

Our oldest litanies are Psalm 118:1-4 and Psalm 136. The first Christian litany probably originated in Antioch in the fourth century and spread through the Eastern and Western churches. For more information on litanies and specifically those in use at King's Chapel see section on Litanies in Components of Worship.

Liturgy – The Greek word, *leitourgeia*, meaning "service," originally meant a work undertaken by a rich citizen for the benefit of a city or country. A wealthy person might finance public games, the building of a stadium, the construction of a fleet, or the celebration of religious rites in a temple. Christians used this word to describe their worship services. For Orthodox Christians, "the liturgy" refers to the Sunday Eucharist.

GLOSSARY

Manual – This term from Latin meant "a book that could be held in the hand (*manus*)." A manual was a book that told the priest how to administer the sacraments.

Mar Thoma Church – A household of churches in southern India that worship according to ancient Syrian traditions modified by Anglican practice. Legend has it that St. Thomas, the disciple of Christ (John 20:26-28), traveled to India in 52 CE, landing on the Malabar Coast and there founding seven churches. Presently a number of Mar Thoma congregations worship in the Americas and Europe, wherever Indian Christians have settled.

Maronite – A community of churches bearing the name of a fourth-century saint, St. Maro. This household of churches was excommunicated at the Council of Constantinople in the year 680. In the twelfth century, like other Uniate churches, they chose to come under the authority of the See of Rome, but kept their own liturgy and prayer books.

Matins – Originally a midnight office inherited from the vigil services of the early church, this service became the first service of the day for those monasteries where the monks rose at 2:00 or 3:00 a.m., as they still do in Cistercian and other strictly observant monasteries. Like other offices, matins consists of psalms, a lesson, a chant, and brief prayers.

Michaelmas – September 29 is the feast day assigned to St. Michael, the principal archangel, who is still honored with a mass on this day. In the northern hemisphere this date may still be the occasion for harvest festivals. English universities and law courts call their fall session, "the Michaelmas term."

GLOSSARY

Missal – A book with all the instructions and text needed for the celebration of the mass. Such books began to appear in the tenth century and combined the five separate books that priests had previously used. See Sacramentary.

Monastery – This word describes the buildings and/or community of a religious order. Although the word originally referred to a male or a female order, it now usually refers to an order of monks.

Mozarabic – This word describes the rich liturgies of the Catholic church in Spain that were abandoned when Pope Alexander II (1061–1073) forbade any local and provincial liturgies differing from those of Rome. At that time, however, a clever Spanish cardinal received permission to continue the Mozarabic rites in a small chapel in the cathedral in Toledo. They survive to this day at that chapel, as well as in two prayers in the King's Chapel prayer book, one on page 39 and the other on page 117.

Nones – This is the last of "the Little Hours," the three midday offices observed at 9:00 a.m., noon, and 3:00 p.m. in convents and monasteries. In the busy life of these institutions it is often said after the principal mass in the morning or at 3:00 p.m. by a member of the community while the others work or rest. (Acts 3:1) In the time of Jesus, 9:00 a.m., noon, and 3:00 p.m. were known as the third, sixth, and ninth hours.

Office – Any of the daily services sung or said in Christian abbeys and cathedrals.

Ordinance – The Oxford English Dictionary defines ordinance as "a practise or useage authoritatively enjoined or prescribed, especially a religious or ceremonial observance." James Freeman borrowed this word to replace the word "sacrament," which meant a divinely sanctioned liturgical action or service.

GLOSSARY

Pascha – This is the Greek translation of the Hebrew *pesach*. Both words mean "a passing over." The first Christians saw themselves as the new Israel, children of a new covenant that God had made with them through their Messiah, Jesus Christ. Thus the Jewish festival of liberation became the Christian festival of salvation. We see this faith in an ancient hymn attributed to St. John of Damascus (c. 675–754), which combines the themes of Passover and spring.

> Come, ye faithful, raise the strain of triumphant gladness;
> God hath brought his Israel into joy from sadness;
> Loosed from Pharoah's bitter yoke Jacob's sons and daughters;
> Led them with unmoistened foot through the Red Sea waters.
>
> 'Tis the spring of souls today; Christ hath burst his prison,
> And from three days sleep in death as a sun hath risen;
> All the winter of our sins, long and dark, is flying
> From his light, to whom we give laud and praise undying.

Most non-English speaking congregations still call the day of resurrection by its original name, *Pascha*.

Passion – Taken from the Latin word for "suffering," *passio*, this word refers to the drama of Christ's suffering, which includes his arrest in the garden, the trials before Caiaphas and Pilate, his flogging, his carrying the cross to Golgotha, and finally his crucifixion there.

Pentecost – A Greek word meaning "fiftieth." Pentecost in Judaism was the fiftieth day after Passover, and the day when the first fruits from the spring harvest were reaped and blessed. (Deuteronomy 16:9-15) Later this agricultural festival became the occasion to celebrate God's giving of the law to Moses on Mount Sinai. (Exodus 19-20)

The Christian Pentecost is the birthday of the church. Acts 2 describes how the holy Spirit descended upon the disciples on the day of

GLOSSARY

the Jewish Pentecost, fifty days after Christ's resurrection. An occasion for baptisms and rich ceremonies, Pentecost was for many years Christendom's second most important holy day, and may still be in some churches. The second half of the church year, the weeks between Pentecost and the first Sunday in Advent, are known as the Pentecost season. See also Whitsunday.

Pharisee – The name in Hebrew means "those who have set themselves apart." Pharisees were pious Jews who lived in Israel, faithfully following the commandments of the Torah, teaching them to lapsed worshipers, and helping them to obey the Law.

The New Testament connects the Pharisees with the Sadducees, but they were two opposing religious parties. Pharisees were popular, moderate, critical of Herod and Rome, and located in towns and villages. They accepted the Prophets and Writings as scripture and believed in the resurrection and angels.

The Sadducees were aristocratic, conservative supporters of Herod and Rome, and were centered in the Temple at Jerusalem. They accepted only the written Torah and denied the existence of angels and the resurrection. Since the Sadducees were centered in Jerusalem and the Temple, they were killed or scattered when the Roman army, while crushing a Jewish rebellion in 70 CE, destroyed the Temple and much of the city.

By contrast, at that time, the members of the Pharisaic party were already living in Jewish communities throughout the Mediterranean world. With the Temple destroyed and the Sadducees scattered, the Pharisees became the political and religious leaders of Jewish communities. Rabbis in our time continue the work of the Pharisees, teaching the Law and applying it to the lives of their congregations.

GLOSSARY

Preface – A preface is a short paragraph to be read or sung before the *Sursum Corda* ("Lift up your hearts") and *Sanctus* ("Holy, holy, holy") in Holy Communion.

On ordinary Sundays the usual preface, "Therefore, with angels and archangels ..." is said. On such days as Christmas, Easter, and Pentecost the minister reads a preface specific to that festival.

Prime – The second morning office appointed to be sung or said daily at 6:00 a.m. This service began in the Bethlehem church in 395, according to St. John Cassian (360–435).

Proper – A prayer, chant, or set of Bible verses appropriate to a given day or season in the church year.

Prophets – The second section of the Jewish scriptures includes the three major (longer) prophetic texts (Isaiah, Jeremiah, and Ezekiel) and those of the twelve minor (shorter) texts (Daniel through Malachi). The section also includes the historical books: Joshua, Judges, I and II Samuel, and I and II Kings, since they tell the stories of the prophets Elijah, Elisha, and Nathan. All the books in this prophetic section were accepted as scripture after the return of the exiles from Babylon in 538 BCE.

Psalter – The book of Psalms or any collection of psalms, even if incomplete.

Rubric – An instruction inserted into the text of a liturgy directing what is to be said or done at that point. It is often printed in red and derives its name from the Latin *rubor*, *rubris* meaning "dark red."

Sabaoth – Not to be confused with the word Sabbath, this word was first used to describe God as the commander of a mighty army, i.e. "Lord of hosts." Later it came to mean the heavenly panoply of angels and archangels who praise God. It is found in the *Te Deum*.

GLOSSARY

Sabbath – From the Hebrew word *shabbat*, meaning "intermission" or "rest." It is the seventh day of the week following six days of work. After six days of creation God rests, and, therefore, the third commandment directs the Hebrew people to rest as well.

Sacrament – The Latin *sacramentum* meant a soldier's oath of loyalty. The Latin New Testament used this word to translate the Greek word, *mysterion*. Although in classical Greek *mysterion* meant rites known only to the members of a cult, in the church it meant the mystery of God's will, which is both hidden and revealed, both known and unknown. See Ephesians 3:9, Colossians 1:26 and 4:3, and I Timothy 3:16.

St. Augustine defined a sacrament as "the visible sign of invisible grace" and "a sign of a sacred thing." Combining these phrases, the Anglican catechism defines a sacrament as "the outward sign of an inward and invisible grace." A sacrament, therefore, is a ritual that embodies and perpetuates our union with God in the life of the Christian community.

Peter Lombard in the twelfth century defined the seven sacraments now accepted by the Roman Catholic Church: Baptism, Confirmation, Eucharist, Penance, Extreme Unction, Ordination, and Matrimony. Most Protestants recognize only Baptism and the Eucharist as sacraments, since Jesus specifically directed his disciples to perform these two actions. (Matthew 28:19 and Luke 22:17-19) James Freeman and his parishioners, averse to priestly language and practice, used the word "ordinance" instead of "sacrament."

Sacramentary – A service book in use until the 1200s that included the text of the mass except for the chants and the New Testament readings. To celebrate the mass a local priest needed several books: a sacramentary, a collection of Gospel readings, a collection of Epistle readings, a manual, and a book of chants.

Sadducee – See Pharisee.

GLOSSARY

Sanctus – The *Sanctus* is the brief hymn of praise beginning "holy, holy, holy," that precedes the prayers in the Eucharist. These opening words are the hymn the seraphim sang in the temple. (Isaiah 6:3) The *Sanctus* concludes with the acclamation of the crowds who greeted Jesus as he entered Jerusalem, "Blessed is he who comes in the name of the Lord." (Matthew 21:9) As early as the year 92, Clement, bishop of Rome (88–99 CE), reports hearing the *Sanctus* during the mass. Therefore it must be one of the oldest parts of the Eucharistic liturgy.

Sanhedrin – From about 300 BCE to 400 CE, the Sanhedrin was the supreme court on religious matters for Jews both in Israel and the whole Mediterranean world. At first based in Jerusalem, it also served as a civil court for that city. The Sanhedrin controlled the finances, services, and other activities of the Temple.

When the Roman army destroyed the Temple in 70 CE, the scholars and rabbis of the Pharisaic party re-established the Sanhedrin in Javneh, sixteen miles south of Jaffa. This court continued to adjudicate religious and judicial issues for Jews until the Roman government, by then largely Christian, dissolved it in the fifth century.

Sarum – This is the old Latin name for Salisbury, the city whose cathedral set the standards for the liturgies and ceremonies of the churches of England, Wales, and Ireland before the Reformation. In 1547 Sarum's authority was confirmed by a royal decree. The services at Sarum provided Cranmer and his prayer book collaborators with much of the material they used in the 1549 and 1552 prayer books.

Septuagesima – The third Sunday before Lent.

Septuagint – Some two centuries before Jesus, Jewish scholars in Alexandria made the definitive translation of the Jewish scriptures into the common (*koine*) Greek, by then the common language of the Mediterranean

GLOSSARY

world. This translation was called the Septuagint (meaning the seventy) because legend had it that seventy scholars accomplished this.

Such a translation was needed for the large number of Jews who had fled famine, poverty, and lack of opportunity in their homeland to find a better life in Egypt, Greece, Rome, Syria, and Asia Minor, which is present-day Turkey. In time these Jews forgot their native Hebrew or Aramaic and read and spoke only common Greek.

Prior to this translation most Jews considered only the Torah and Prophets to be their scriptures. But the Septuagint included not only the Writings but most of the Apocrypha as well.

Seraphim – See Angel.

Sin – Sin is a threatening word both in and outside the church. In recent history it has connoted harsh, unforgiving judgment for such pleasures as drinking, dancing, and making love, as well as for cruelty, greed and destructiveness. During the Middle Ages the Christian theologians distinguished between venial sins (not damnable) and mortal sins, (damnable, unless forgiven.) King's Chapel parishioners have suggested replacing "sin" with such words as error, wrongdoing, thoughtlessness, or selfishness. In all these instances sin is seen as an individual action.

Christian theology teaches that sin is the universal condition of all humanity before it becomes the act of an individual. Theologian Piet Smoulders defines sin as " a deep-cutting egotism in the inmost chambers of the heart, a *curvitas* that turns chiefly upon itself." The natural disposition to act in one's self-interest is essential to our survival, but almost inevitably it moves to excess. This disposition is dangerous in a single person, but is far more dangerous in a group, whether that group be a faction or an institution such as a church, a corporation, or a city, state, or nation.

The church teaches that every one of us has this "deep-cutting egotism" as part of his or her nature, and that every one of us is embedded in self-serving institutions. For this reason in both Holy Communion and

GLOSSARY

Morning and Evening Prayer we say aloud and together a prayer of confession. As we say these prayers we have little time to recall our personal failings, but we can always acknowledge our common condition.

Confession, whether general or specific, makes sense only if we believe that we can be freed from sin. When the Bible speaks of God's forgiveness, it tells us that we are promised that freedom despite our sin and guilt. God calls us to freedom and has given us a remedy. It is called repentance.

The Greek word *metánoia*, which we translate as repentance, means changing one's mind. The church teaches that a new view of ourselves, our neighbors, and our world, provides this remedy. Repentance requires genuine contrition for our misdoings, confession of these misdoings to an appropriate person, and some form of restitution. From these three acts comes freedom. Those in Alcoholics Anonymous know how true this is.

Synagogue – This word is the Greek translation of the Hebrew *bet kenesset*, meaning the house of assembly, that is, the gathering place for prayer and study that could and can be found in every observant Jewish community. Synagogue worship in the time of Jesus consisted of readings from the Torah and Prophets, prayers and psalms. Luke 4:16 describes Jesus reading from the prophecy of Isaiah in the Nazareth synagogue. Mark 1:21 describes him teaching in the Capernaum synagogue.

A synagogue was as much a house of study as a house of prayer and sometimes might even be the scene of judicial reviews and trials. The New England counterpart to a synagogue is the meetinghouse. For the origins of the synagogue, read the opening of the Introduction to Morning and Evening Prayer.

Surplice – A white liturgical vestment, originally of linen. When worn at mid-length by choir members it is often called a cotta. It is worn at full length by clergy, crucifers, acolytes, and other lay assistants.

GLOSSARY

Taize – This is the name of a French village in Burgundy where a small, independent, ecumenical, monastic order was founded in 1940. The one hundred monks who now comprise this community create and send out many forms of lovely worship, mostly hymns and prayers, that are used in churches around the world. Taize is host to more than a hundred thousand young people who come year-round to pray, worship, and receive religious instruction.

Tate and Brady – In 1696 Nicholas Tate and Nahum Brady, two Irish Protestant clergymen, produced a new versification of the psalms to serve as a hymnal for the Church of England. At that time congregations sang only psalms as well as chants from the prayer book. Almost all psalms were set to Long Meter, consisting of four lines with eight beats to a line, or Common Meter, consisting of four lines with alternating beats of eight and six. King's Chapel adopted the Tate and Brady Psalter in 1713.

Temple – This term refers always to the Temple in Jerusalem, the ritual center for Jewish worship for about a thousand years. Solomon (970–933 BCE) built the First Temple, which was completed in 957 BCE. I Kings 8:1-21 describes the dedication ceremony. Ecclesiasticus 50:1-21 describes the sacrifices that took place in the Temple. It was destroyed in 586 BCE by the Babylonian army under Nebuchadnezzar.

The Second Temple, dedicated about 520 BCE and less glorious than the first, was built by the exiles who returned from Babylon. The prophets Haggai and Zechariah urged them in this undertaking. The Second Temple, although turned into a pagan sanctuary by the armies of Antiochus Epiphanies, king of Syria, was rededicated in 164 BCE.

This Second Temple was supplanted in 20 BCE by the great Third Temple, which Herod the Great (37–4 BCE) built in just a few years. It stood for less than a century and was destroyed in 70 CE by Roman armies sent to suppress a rebellion. The platform of the Third Temple still stands. It is part of the Wailing Wall, where Jews pray to this day.

GLOSSARY

Terce – The first of the Little Hours, the short daily offices read at the third, sixth and ninth hours, that is, 9:00 a.m., noon and 3:00 p.m. The book of Acts (3:1 and 10:9) describes Peter and John praying at these hours.

Testament – This word is a translation of the Greek *diatheke*, a word meaning "covenant," which Christians used to describe their scriptures. The scriptures inherited from Judaism were, therefore, "the old covenant," and their own scriptures "the new covenant." For Christians the first witnessed to the covenant God made with Judaism and the second to the covenant God made with them through Jesus Christ.

Torah – This word, meaning "the teaching," is the most sacred text of Jewish scripture. It consists of the books of Genesis, Exodus, Leviticus, Numbers, and Deuteronomy. These are also called the *Pentateuch* (Greek for "the five scrolls") or the Law. On the Torah all other Jewish scripture rests.

The Torah became scripture in 622 BCE when the high priest Hilkiah found "the book of the covenant" (namely, the scrolls containing the Torah) in the Temple. He took them to King Josiah who accepted them as God's word to his people. II Kings 22:3-13 and 23:1-3 describe this event. Nehemiah 8:1-12 describes the first public reading of the Torah.

The Torah is also known as the written Torah. It was followed in later centuries by extensive unwritten commentary known as the Mishnah or "the instruction," also called the oral Torah. Still later came the Gemara, a commentary on the Mishnah. Both the Mishnah and the Gemara were eventually incorporated into the Talmud (200 BCE–500 CE), the authoritative body of Jewish scriptural commentary and law.

Transfiguration – This term describes the revealing of Jesus as divine to three disciples, Peter, James, and John. (Mark 9: 2-9) Christians soon began to celebrate this event on Mount Tabor, the traditional site of its occurrence, and in the fourth century built a church there. By the year 1000 the Transfiguration had become a universal feast in the church.

GLOSSARY

Translations – The reading of the Bible is one of the high points in a Christian worship service. But which Bible translation will the congregation hear?

For more than three centuries no one in English-speaking churches would have raised this question. Protestant congregations would have heard the King James Bible, published in 1611, and Catholics would have heard the Douay-Rheims Version, published in 1582 and 1610.

In 1900 this began to change. In that year a group of scholars produced a revision of the King James Bible called the American Standard Version. This translation never challenged the authority of the King James, but it was the basis for a later translation that did. In 1948 and in 1952 a group of American scholars produced the Revised Standard Version, which became the definitive text for many churches and seminaries in this country and the basis for other translations, both Catholic and Protestant, including the currently popular New Revised Standard Version.

In addition to the RSV, other new English translations have appeared in the last fifty years. In 2011 Wikipedia listed more than a hundred of these. What brought about this spate of translations?

In the first place, language evolves. Words commonly used three centuries ago are either no longer spoken or have changed their meaning. "Feeble-minded" no longer means "fainthearted," "reins" no longer means "kidneys," and "leasing" no longer means "lies."

Phrases change too. "We do you to wit" does not tell us "we want you to know." "Let no man seek his own, but another's wealth" does not mean "Let each seek the good of his neighbor." More than a thousand words and phrases in the King James Bible are now archaic. We now need translations not only from Greek, Latin, and Hebrew, but from Old English as well.

Something else has changed. Archeological digs and the discovery of historical documents have taught us more about the ancient Near Eastern world than our ancestors knew. Such discoveries have enabled us to understand the context of life in the villages, cities, courts, and temples of Rome, Greece, Egypt, Asia Minor, and the Holy Land.

GLOSSARY

A third event has changed biblical scholarship, namely, the discovery of ancient biblical documents. In some cases this was due to the publication of manuscripts that had long been held in private collections or monasteries. For example, the Codex Vaticanus, a fourth century collection of some Old Testament books in Greek, did not appear in English until 1869. In other cases, some manuscripts were actually found. One example is *The Teaching of the Twelve Apostles*, the oldest extant Christian catechism with instruction on baptism, fasting, daily prayer, and how to celebrate the Eucharist. It appeared in English in 1884, and two prayers from it were incorporated in a Holy Communion service in the 1918 King's Chapel prayer book.

One of the big postwar finds was the Naj Hammadi library, a collection of papyri containing more than forty manuscripts written by various Gnostic authors. Prior to this discovery in 1945 we knew the Gnostic writings only as described by their Christian opponents. Now we can read the originals. These documents help us better to understand the heresies early Christian theologians were attacking.

The fourth and final need for new translations was the very familiarity of the King James and Douay-Rheims versions. Congregations knew the texts so well they did not feel the power of the faith that produced these texts. C. S. Lewis put this point well, when he wrote: "We must get away from the Authorized Version, if for no other reason because it is so beautiful and solemn. Beauty exalts, but beauty also lulls ... the Book becomes blunted or disarmed, and we may only sigh with tranquil veneration when we ought to burn with shame or be struck dumb with terror."

For these four reasons, and perhaps others as well, we now have a number of translations of the Bible, some colloquial, some scholarly, and some based on the King James. Interlinear Bibles show the English words next to the Greek or Hebrew words they translate.

Most translations were done by teams of scholars. The King James translators relied on documents in Hebrew, Greek, and Latin. Contemporary scholars work from many documents in several languages

GLOSSARY

including Syriac, Aramaic, and Akkadian. They compare these documents and must decide which one to follow in translating a particular passage.

Translators must also choose the right meaning of a word for the passage they are translating. For example, in translating the Hebrew word, *alma*, the King James translators chose the meaning "virgin" and so Isaiah 7:14 read, "Behold, a virgin shall conceive." *Alma* also means a young woman of marriageable age, presumably a virgin, but the specific Hebrew word for virgin is *b'tulah*. Therefore, the New Revised Standard Version translated *alma* "a young woman" and so the same verse in the NRSV reads, "Look, the young woman is with child."

One more example of translation difficulties is found in John 1:1, which reads in most translations "In the beginning was the Word." But the Greek word *logos*, translated "Word," is rich in meanings. Clarence Jordan translates it as "Idea" and J. B. Phillips translates it as "the Divine Expression." The Chinese Bible says, "In the beginning was the Tao."

We can sympathize with translators who must not only find the correct context for a passage, the correct meaning of a word, but also the right expression in English to convey both the literal meaning and the emotional sense of the original.

So we return to the question: which Bible should we use? There is no one correct translation. Sometimes the majesty of the King James is needed. Sometimes the literal precision of the New Revised Standard is best. Sometimes the blunt colloquialism in the *Cotton Patch Bible* is right for, say, the letters of St. Paul. Sometimes we find a happy balance between majesty and literal truth in such a translation as the Jerusalem Bible. The worship leader needs at least a small shelf of Bibles to choose from. But what a privilege to choose from many and not be bound to one!

Transubstantiation – Still the official teaching of the Roman Catholic Church on Christ's presence in the Eucharist, this doctrine is based on Aristotle's distinction between the substance, meaning the actual reality of a thing, and its accident, that is, its appearance. In the Eucharist the bread and wine appear to be only bread and wine, but actually (substantially)

GLOSSARY

they are the body and blood of Christ. This doctrine was adopted at the Fourth Lateran Council (1215), confirmed at the Council of Trent (1545 – 1563), and reaffirmed at the Second Vatican Council in 1962. So strong was the reaction of the Church of England against this teaching that in 1673 Parliament passed a law stating that anyone aspiring to a civil or military office had to take an oath swearing that they did not believe in the doctrine of transubstantiation.

Trinity – See Doctrine under Components of Worship in the text.

Uniate – This term describes those Eastern churches that have remained in or renewed communion with Rome. By terms of their agreement with the Vatican they are allowed to keep their own languages, liturgies, and canon law. Parish priests, but not bishops, may marry. They baptize by immersion and congregations receive communion in both kinds (the bread and the wine). Uniat churches are found primarily in Syria, Armenia, Romania, Poland, and Ukraine.

Unitarianism – See Doctrine under Components of Worship in the text.

Versicles – A set of responsive sentences said between celebrant and the congregation, such as "The Lord be with you," and the response, "And with thy spirit."

Vespers – Originally this was an office said or sung during the night vigil before the Sunday Eucharist. It was then called the *Lucernarium* because candles were needed for its celebration. During such a service several psalms are said or sung with antiphons followed by a lesson, the *Magnificat*, an evening collect, and a final blessing. Parts of the ancient vespers survive in our service of Evening Prayer and Evensong.

Vigil – A nocturnal service, lasting all night or into the early morning, often ending in the Eucharist. The early Christians held such services perhaps because they believed that Christ's second coming would take place in darkness. Vigils are still held before such holy days as Easter and Pentecost in many churches. Orthodox churches hold vigils every Saturday evening before the Sunday Eucharist.

Vulgate – This translation of Greek texts into Latin became the authoritative scripture of the Roman Catholic Church until the Second Vatican Council in the early 1960s. St. Jerome (c. 331–420) took twenty years to make this translation. Since he wrote this, not in classical Latin, but in the common speech of ordinary people, the *vulgus*, it acquired the name Vulgate.

Western, West – Until the Protestant Reformation this term referred to all Christian churches in Western Europe loyal to Rome. Since then it has come to mean all churches—Protestant, Catholic, Evangelical, and otherwise in Europe and the Americas.

Whitsunday – The English name for Pentecost, so called perhaps because those to be baptized on this day wore white. Augustinian canon John Mirk gave another reason in a sermon he preached in 1400: "Good men and wimmen, this day is called Wytsonday by cause the holy ghost bought wytte and wisdom into Crists dyscyples…"

Whitsunday was a festive day, sometimes a festive week, in pre-industrial England. Even in the twentieth century, it was celebrated with fairs, pageants, plays, races, walks, wakes, Morris dancing, and a Whitson ale. These traditions continue in some English parishes.

GLOSSARY

Writings – The Writings are the third section of the Jewish scriptures and the last to be accepted into the canon in 90 CE by the council of elders, possibly assembled in Javneh, a town sixteen miles south of Jaffa. They contain the Psalms, Lamentations, the Song of Songs, the wisdom books (Proverbs, Job, and Ecclesiastes), the histories (Ruth, I and II Chronicles, Esther, Ezra, and Nehemiah,) and the apocalypse known as Daniel.

Several portions of the Writings are read at major Jewish festivals. Ruth is read at the spring harvest; Ecclesiastes at Sukkot, the fall harvest; Esther at Purim; the Song of Songs at Passover; and Lamentations at Tish-be-Av, which mourns the destruction of the First Temple in 586 BCE and the Third Temple in 70 CE.

PORTRAIT BY GERLACH FLICKE, 1545.

Thomas Cranmer, Archbishop of Canterbury, led the creation
of the first Anglican prayer book based on the new Protestant
liturgy for King Edward VI in 1549. It has been adapted
over the years by Anglicans and Episcopalians as well
as for the Christian Unitarians at King's Chapel.

ACKNOWLEDGMENTS

It takes a village to raise not only a child, but a book like this. First of all it takes ancestors, including two millennia of priests, bishops, theologians, and worshipers who have kept Christian worship alive and strong.

It takes a library, including the rich liturgical resource in the 1979 Episcopal *Book of Common Prayer*, to which I am deeply indebted, as well as two commentaries, Massey Shepard's on the 1928 American *Book of Common Prayer* and Marion Hatchett's on the 1979 revision.

It takes such places as St. Margaret's Convent and Glastonbury Abbey where the hospitality and prayers of the nuns in one and the brothers at the other provided an environment in which I did intense and productive work.

And it takes such people as the Rev. Joy Fallon, my successor at King's Chapel. She encouraged me and supported the publication of this text. Her interim predecessor, the Rev. Dianne Arakawa, provided strong encouragement and support and started me writing again after too long a pause.

Parishioners Cliff Allen, Christine Bergstrom, Ric Holt, the Rev. Christine Jaronski, Carol Kemp, William Park, Betsy Peterson, and Carolyn Russ read drafts of this commentary. Todd Lee, the Rev. John Bunyan, and the Rev. Jed Mannis provided extensive corrections and improvements to the text. Book designer Victoria Sax transformed the text into pages, and King's Chapel's Historic Program Director Faye Charpentier assisted with photography and images. I thank all of them for their contributions.

My first editor, Lil Copan, graciously turned a raw, unfinished text into an intelligible manuscript. Those who have worked with her know how fortunate I was to have her help.

Parishioner Karen Cord Taylor, my second editor, volunteered her experience, judgment, good humor, and uncounted hours and days of her time in the rewriting, editing, proofreading, and production that this text required.

Through this long endeavor my wife, Faith, endured my complaints, soliloquies, and discouragement with a healing sense of reality.

Finally, I want to thank the congregation at King's Chapel, who taught me what it means to worship in a prayer book tradition.

INDEX

INDEX

INDEX

INDEX

INDEX

BIBLICAL INDEX

	PAGE			PAGE
Acts			**Corinthians, II**	
1:5–8	64		3:4-6	118
2	53, 71, 156, 219		4:16-18	186
			10:10	186
2:1-10	116		11:23-29	186
2:14-36	156		15:9	186
2:38; 10:48	53		12:2-4	186
2:38-39	60		12:7-10	186
2:38, 41; 8:12; 16:15	53		13:14	187
2:42, 46; 20:7a	71		**Daniel**, 3:1-24	29
7:54-60	157		**Deuteronomy**	
8:1	186		5:6-21	132, 201
8:16; 19:5	53		6:4-7	56, 132
9:1-2	186		**Ecclesiastes**, 12:7	109
11:26	19		**Ecclesiasticus**	
16:15, 33; 18:8	54		50:11-21	136
20:7, 71	71, 146		**Ephesians**	
23:12,21	194		3:21	26
Chronicles, II, 20:6	36		4:4-6	60
Colossians, 3:16	122		5:18-19	122
Corinthians, I			6:12	35
1:22	153		**Exodus**	
3:9-10, 12	219		1:1-6	118
5:7-8; 10:16	73		20:2-17	132
11:23-26	70, 81, 118, 204		**Galatians**, 1:13-14	186
			Genesis	
11:24-25	81		9:1-17	118
11:27-29	75		15:15-20	118
11:29-30	133		18:1-14	194
12	194		32:24-30	194
12:13, 27, 26	64		**Hebrews**	
13:9-10, 12	108		8:6-13	118
14:15	122		13:14	108
15:9	186		**Isaiah**	
16:2	146		6:1-3	78
16:22	194		6:1-8	32
22	153		6:3	88
			40:6-8	104
			53:6	23

BIBLICAL INDEX

BIBLICAL INDEX

	PAGE		PAGE
Psalms		136	141, 208
4:8	42	137	136, 141
9:18	42	139	162
19:1	120, 140	139:11-12	45
19:7	140	141	49
20:9	42	144:6	138
22:1, 31:5	136	148-150	208
23, 130	141	**Revelation**	
23, 42, 121, 139	162	1:10	146
23:1	140	3:14	193
24, 132, 150	136	3:20	73
28:9	42	3:20; 22:17	90
30, 130, 131	141	4:8,11; 5:9-10;	
30:8	140	14:13; 15:3-4;	
37:21	140	19:1-2	122
38:3	23	5:12	202
48:6	140	19:1, 3, 4, 6	193
51:1-2	23	14:13	109
51:1-3, 10	43	22:17	73
51:10a, 11	33, 42	**Romans**	
51:15	26	8:38	35
67	30, 44, 50, 202	12:2	82
		16:27	26
83:17	138	**Ruth**, 2:4	33
85:7	33, 42	**Samuel, I**, 2:1-10	32
96:9, 13	26	**Timothy, I**	
98	44	1:15	77
100	30	1:17	26, 202
103:13-14	104	2:1-2	36
113:5-6	36	6:7	104
118	137, 141, 154, 208	**Titus**, 2:12	23
119:164	19		
129	140		
130	111		
130, 137	138		
132:9	42		

Made in the USA
Middletown, DE
14 April 2018